From:
One "Skerkquacious" Sker
to another.

Here's to your
"deviated septum"

Grused Hatter
May 27/83

BRAVE NEW WORDS

BRAVE NEW WORDS

The newest, funniest, and most original dictionary in the world

BILL "SESQUILINGUAL" SHERK

Illustrated by Leah Taylor

1979
Doubleday Canada Limited, Toronto, Ontario
Doubleday & Company, Inc., Garden City, New York

Copyright © 1979 by Bill Sherk
Library of Congress Catalog Card Number 79-7455

First edition
Printed in Canada by The Alger Press Limited
Designed by Robert Burgess Garbutt

"Elephant Stew," by Jack Rickel, is from the *Mark Twain Library Cookbook* Volume Two, copyright © 1976 by the Mark Twain Library Association, Inc., Redding, Connecticut, and is reprinted by permission.

"Roget's Girl," by John Robert Colombo, is reprinted from *Variable Cloudiness* (Toronto: Hounslow Press, 1977) by permission of the author.

Canadian Cataloguing in Publication Data

Sherk, Bill, 1942–
   Brave new words

Bibliography: p. 171
ISBN 0-385-15552-2 bd. ISBN 0-385-15331-7 pa.

1. Words, New—English—Dictionaries. 2. English language—Dictionaries. I. Title.

PE1630.S46   427   C79-094509-6

to Joyce, Jeffrey and Juliana

Introduction

Nowhere else in the world will you find a dictionary like this one. From cover to cover its pages are packed with a succulent array of juicy linguistic morsels. One hundred freshly minted words are about to parade themselves right before your dazzled eyes!

But first, a few pages filled with flamboyant phraseology to whet your appetite . . .

A Linguistic Bombshell!

Most dictionaries are heavy, stuffy affairs guaranteed to put you to sleep faster than you can say "Forty winks." But Brave New Words is light, lean, streamlined, and full of punch, pizazz, and razzle-dazzle! Where else can you find words like *g'orch* and *spork, rexile* and *riggafrutch, fuzztache* and *foof, klickage* and *kangamungle, Norsex* and *niblings*, as well as *swinephone, sexophile, unikini, Polequator, forelog, foon,* and *ugloo*—not to mention the word that gave birth to this one-of-a-kind dictionary in the first place: *sesquilingual* (sĕs-kwĭ-LĬNG-gwăl)?

Brave New What???

This book was nearly half written before I suddenly realized it didn't have a title. I quickly drew up a list of a dozen or more possible titles ranging all the way from *The Sherktionary* to *Word Coiners on the Loose*. But nothing on the list seemed to have the short, quick punch I was looking for.

Then one day at school between History classes, I mentioned the problem to a fellow teacher named Bob Brown (the same Bob Brown who coined *alphadef,* the first entry in this book). Brown stared at the floor for about five seconds, then said, "Why not call it Brave New Words?"

Eureka! I knew right away how Archimedes must have felt when he discovered his famous principle for the displacement of water. The search for a title was over.

Brown's brainstorm was, of course, inspired by *Brave New World*, a futuristic novel by Aldous Huxley published in 1932. But where did

Introduction

Huxley get *his* title? From the Bard of Avon himself, William Shakespeare! Turn to *The Tempest*, Act V, Scene 1, and you'll find Miranda, daughter of the Duke of Milan, gushing with eloquence:

> O, wonder!
> How many goodly creatures are there here!
> How beauteous mankind is! O brave new world,
> That hath such people in't!

If Shakespeare came back to life today, you'd see him rushing into the nearest bookstore to snap up a copy of *Brave New Words*. Why? Because Shakespeare was a passionate lover of new words. He fathered hundreds of them. According to Willard Espy, in *An Almanac of Words at Play*, "of the 1700 words said to have been coined by Shakespeare . . . hundreds have become fixtures. A few attributed to him: Assassination, suspicious, barefaced, bump, castigate, critical, countless, denote, dwindle, eventful, foppish, fretful, gnarled, hurry, impartial, lapse, laughable, lonely, leapfrog, misplaced, monumental, sportive."

Believe it or not, several faintly disguised references to *Brave New Words* (this very book!) can be found scattered throughout Shakespeare's plays. Hamlet's soliloquy, for example:

> To coin, or not to coin: that is the question:
> Whether 'tis nobler in the mind not to suffer
> The slings and arrows of outraged lexicographers,
> Or to take arms against a stack of dictionaries,
> And by coining obsolete them?

Published in the Nick of Time

If we include the three years, three months and sixteen days I spent reading *The Webster Universal Dictionary* from cover to cover (see *alphomeg* for details), then *Brave New Words* has been five years in the making. And it's now coming out in the nick of time! Even if it accomplishes nothing else, *Brave New Words* will help magazine editor John Kalbfleisch to get a good night's sleep:

> Lately I've been having this awful, recurring nightmare that one day I will stumble across the news scoop of the century, a story to make Watergate about as interesting as a change in the Bank of Canada prime rate and me as famous as Woodward and

Introduction ix

Bernstein together—but the words to tell it won't exist. Literally. There I am, copy paper in my typewriter, presses ready to roll, frantic editors howling like banshees for my deathless prose; but no words come because the ones I need have not been invented yet. ["Could You Say That in Canadian, Please?" *Weekend,* October 16, 1976.]

An Overnight Success

Unlike other dictionaries, which only include words already in use, *Brave New Words* has the audacity to print words, most of which are not yet in use anywhere! Such linguistic boldness brings its own rewards, not the least of which is the satisfaction of seeing new words get into circulation fast!!!

But even *Brave New Words* would be hard-pressed to match the speed with which a certain Russian word joined the English language:

> Perhaps the fastest entry of a word into a dictionary happened in 1957. On October 4 of that year, the Russians sent the world's first satellite, Sputnik I, into orbit around the earth. An editor in New York saw the word in a newspaper delivered to his desk. He grabbed the phone and called a printing plant in the Midwest where his company's new dictionary was just about ready to be printed. "Stop the press!" he shouted. Over the long distance phone, he dictated a definition of the word. One day later, *sputnik* appeared in a dictionary and became part of the English language. [Robert Kraske, *The Story of the Dictionary.*]

Today, Canada—Tomorrow, the World!

As you romp through the pages of *Brave New Words,* an inescapable fact will sooner or later strike you right between the eyes: all the new words in this book have been coined by Canadians. (Even the one exception—*slantendicularist*—was coined by a lady in Michigan who was born in Canada.)

The reason for this is simple. Living as I do in Toronto, Ontario, I first began soliciting new words for this book through articles in local newspapers. In his article "Inventive Dictionary Should Please Canuckophiles" (April 12, 1977), William French of *The Globe and Mail* in Toronto helped to spread the word:

Introduction

Several international dictionaries in recent years have taken notice of such specifically Canadian words and phrases as chinook, igloo, baby bonus, beer parlor and snowmobile. But the dictionary now being prepared by Bill Sherk of York University may be the first entirely made up of words invented by Canadians, and it will give some of them a chance for immortality. . . .

Sherk is soliciting new words from the general public for his dictionary, and promises to include the name of the person who coined the word beside each entry. The challenge should prove irresistible, and undoubtedly one or more of the following will be submitted—polyglib, a politician fluent in several languages; piscadoor, the entrance to a fish plant; mygrain, a bore from the prairies; theolog, a chaplain in a lumber camp; hortense, an uptight prostitute.

And the word for Sherk, clearly, is neologophile.

Hot on the heels of that and similar articles, my telephone began ringing with invitations to appear as a guest on local and cross-Canada radio and television. Cards and letters bearing new words soon began arriving from coast to coast.

Meanwhile, other new words began pouring in from a much more immediate source: from my History students at North Toronto Collegiate and from my Word Power students at York University's Centre for Continuing Education in Toronto. I soon discovered I had enough material from strictly Canadian sources for Volume One of *Brave New Words*.

If you live outside Canada, don't feel left out. Preparation for Volume Two is now underway and more new words are eagerly invited from anywhere in the English-speaking world.

If you come up with a hot new word, fill out the convenient Word Card at the back of this book and pop it into the nearest mailbox. Your word and your name could hit the pages of our next edition.

A Crash Course on How to Invent Words

When sitting down to coin a new word, you can plan your attack from several different directions. You can steal a word from a foreign language (sputnik, for example), although this method is not terribly inventive since the word already exists outside of English.

Introduction xi

Many of the entries in *Brave New Words* (such as *dek, covivant,* and *menuographer*) have been formed by giving a fresh new twist to some old Latin or Greek roots. Many other entries are portmanteau words (made by taking two existing words such as *lunch* and *supper* and slamming them together to produce *lupper*—the afternoon equivalent of brunch). Such origins are not surprising. The words in the English language are now coming of age, getting together, and producing offspring in an unbridled orgy of linguistic reproduction.

If acronyms turn you on, you'll be delighted to know that this is the book that gives you *foof* for Fine Old Ontario Family (also comes in handy in Ohio, Oklahoma, Oregon, and on the Hawaiian island of Oahu). Another acronym snugly ensconced in the pages ahead is *pwelgas,* a handy little word to help you keep the Seven Deadly Sins at your fingertips: Pride, Wrath, Envy, Lust, Gluttony, Avarice, and Sloth.

If you like onomatopoetic words (they sound like what they mean), you'll love *doonic* and *galoosh.*

André and *sherkquacious* are known as eponyms because each is based on a person's name. Perhaps to find the new word you'd like to coin, you need search no further than your own surname. Then your only problem will be: What new meaning should it have?

Riggafrutch and *gnurn* are two examples of new words born out of spontaneous verbal combustion. Like the goddess Athena bursting in full armour from the head of Zeus, these words have emerged full blown and fully formed from the vocal chords of their creators.

But coining a new word is much like trying to catch a butterfly. The more you try, the more the butterfly flutters just out of reach. But if you stand very still and think about something else, it may land on your shoulder.

If a new word lands on your shoulder, write it down *immediately*—before it slips your mind. And always carry something to write with. We'll never know how many new words have died at birth for lack of a pen or pencil.

Brave New Words for Your Immediate Pleasure

The "brave new words" in this book are not afraid to suffer the slings and arrows of outraged lexicographers. These new words refuse to sleep in someone's filing cabinet, patiently waiting for official blessing from Oxford or Webster. These words are itching for some action right now! No matter where you live in the English-speaking world, you can start using these new words not tomorrow, not next week, but TODAY!

At first, people won't know what you're talking about, but that will only intensify the indescribable verbal pleasure you will derive from letting these words roll off your tongue in an unparalleled display of linguistic oneupmanship.

Just think how fast you'll become the life of the party when you tell the host you're *omnibibulous,* you eat all your food with a *foon,* and you're thinking of buying a *sesquinsula* that sits right on the *Polequator.* Your friends will be amazed, your boss will be impressed, and your local librarian (whose knowledge of words has always overwhelmed you) will be speechless.

Many Are Coined But Few Are Chosen

And now for the question everyone is asking: How many of these new words will catch on to become permanent members of the English language?

The answer can be found in the Gospel according to Saint Matthew, Chapter 13, verses 3-8:

> Behold, a sower went forth to sow; And when he sowed, some seeds fell by the way side, and the fowls came and devoured them up:
>
> Some fell upon stony places, where they had not much earth: and forthwith they sprung up, because they had no deepness of earth:
>
> And when the sun was up, they were scorched; and because they had no root, they withered away.
>
> And some fell among thorns; and the thorns sprung up, and choked them:
>
> But other fell into good ground, and brought forth fruit, some an hundredfold, some sixtyfold, some thirtyfold.

Some of these new words will make it to Oxford and Webster and some won't. But *all* of them have already made it to *Brave New Words.* And all the new words appearing in this book have been selected because they have one thing in common: All of them tickle my fancy.

I hope they tickle yours.

No Absolute Claims

Except for *footle* (which now has a new meaning), all the entries in *Brave New Words* are brand new insofar as they do *not* appear in any of the following dictionaries (or in any other dictionaries I am aware of):

> *The Barnhart Dictionary of New English Since 1963.* Clarence L. Barnhart et al, Editors. Barnhart/Harper & Row, New York, 1973.
>
> *The Doubleday Dictionary.* Sidney I. Landau, Editor in Chief. Doubleday & Company, Inc., Garden City, New York, 1975.
>
> *The Heritage Illustrated Dictionary of the English Language.* International Edition. William Morris, Editor. American Heritage Publishing Co., Inc., and Houghton Mifflin Company, New York, 1973.
>
> *The Oxford English Dictionary.* Twelve Volumes plus Supplements. Sir James Murray et al, Editors. First published at the Clarendon Press, Oxford, 1928.
>
> *The Oxford Illustrated Dictionary.* J. Coulson et al, Editors. Clarendon Press, Oxford, 1975.
>
> *Webster's Third New International Dictionary of the English Language.* Unabridged. Philip Babcock Gove, Editor in Chief. G. & C. Merriam Company, Springfield, Massachusetts, 1966.

Each person (including myself) who has donated a new word to this book claims to be the person who coined it. To the best of my knowledge, each claim is authentic. But in a language as far-flung and widely spoken as English, it's entirely possible for a new word to be coined independently by different people.

If you have proof that any of the main entries in *Brave New Words* first appeared in print somewhere else, please let me know so that proper credit can be given in our next edition.

BILL "SESQUILINGUAL" SHERK
Toronto, Canada
April 1979

Pronunciation Guide

All accented syllables are fully capitalized (as in sĕs-kwĭ-LĬNG-gwăl) to provide a POWERFUL VISUAL IMPACT! Vowels are marked as follows:

Short vowels
ă   as in pat
ĕ   as in pet
ĭ   as in pit
ŏ   as in pot
ŭ   as in putt
o͝o   as in soot

Long vowels
ā   as in raid
ē   as in reed
ī   as in ride
ō   as in rode
yo͞o   as in unicorn
o͞o   as in rude

Pronunciations not covered above are made obvious by their similarity to existing words. For example:

1) *connoizer* (kŏ-NOY-zĕr). NOY rhymes with *boy*.
2) *g'orch* and *spork* rhyme with *cork*.
3) *plouse* rhymes with *house*.
4) *tonguetipitis* (tŭng-tĭ-PIGHT-ĭs). PIGHT rhymes with *might*.

BRAVE NEW WORDS

alphadef

(ĂL-fă-dēf) noun. Rhymes with *belief*.
A new synonym for *dictionary*.
(contraction of *alphasonic definer*—see below)
Coined by Bob Brown, Willowdale, Ontario.

It is only fitting that this dictionary of new words should spring into action with a new synonym for *dictionary* itself. Bob Brown, a Toronto teacher, says the time has come to kick *dictionary* out of the language and replace it with something fresh and exciting. He first suggested *alphasonic definer* (wow!) because a dictionary arranges words alphabetically and shows you how to pronounce and define them. But finding seven syllables too much of a mouthful, Brown shortened his creation to *alphadef*.

If this new word catches on (and people are placing their bets already), the writers of dictionaries will stop calling themselves lexicographers and start calling themselves *alphadefographers* (ăl-fă-dē-FŎG-ră-fěrz). And why not? Like a rear-window defogger in your car, well-written dictionary (oops! . . . a well-written alphadef) blows away the fog surrounding any word you might look up. You could even call the book an *alphadefogger*.

We can thank Latin for giving us *dictionary* (from *dicere*—to say) and Greek for giving us *lexicon* (from *lexis*—word). And we can now thank Bob Brown for giving us *alphadef*.

From now on, the world of words will be known as *alphadefdom*. What other choice have we? *Dictionarydom* sounds dumb and *lexicondom* sounds like a monogrammed prophylactic.

LOOK IT UP!
If you stumble upon a strange new word,
Don't weep and gnash your teeth.
Just smile and say in a cheerful way,
"I'll look it up in my alphadef!"

alphadef

> **SPECIAL NOTICE**
>
> Residents of Prince Albert, Saskatchewan, may prefer to spell this new word alpha*dief* in honour of their most illustrious citizen, the Right Honourable John Diefenbaker ("Dief the Chief"), who served as Canada's thirteenth prime minister from 1957 to 1963. Diefenbaker's command of the English language is legendary. If anyone deserves to have a dictionary named after him, he's the one.
>
> When I wrote to Mr. Diefenbaker, asking his permission to link his name with this new word, his secretary, Beatrice Eligh, replied: "No, Mr. Diefenbaker has no objection to your coining a word using his name in it if you wish to do so. He has asked me to tell you that he has had dogs named after him, but this is the first time a new word has been manufactured around his name!"

alphomeg

(ĂL-fō-měg) noun.
A person who has read a dictionary from cover to cover. "Ah! Just a few more pages and I'll be a full-fledged alphomeg!"
(From *alpha* and *omega*, the first and last letters of the Greek alphabet. Coinage inspired by the Book of Revelations, Chapter 22, verse 13: "I am Alpha and Omega, the beginning and the end, the first and the last.")
Coined by the author.

"You're reading a dictionary from cover to cover? Sherk, you must be crazy!"

Not everyone shared my boundless enthusiasm for the journey I had embarked upon. That journey began shortly after sunrise on Saturday November 10, 1973, in the library of my home in Toronto. I was flipping through my copy of *The Webster Universal Dictionary*, searching for nothing in particular, when suddenly it hit me! For years I had been browsing helter skelter through this book. Why not read all of it—one page a day—from cover to cover?

I grabbed a calendar, checked the size of the dictionary (1205 pages), and figured that if I started right away, I would finish on Saturday February 26, 1977. From *aardvark* to *zyxomma*, the journey would take three years, three months, and 16 days. With pen clutched eagerly in hand to circle all the gems lying single file in my path. I sallied forth in a frenzy of excitement.

Before reaching the bottom of the first page, I found *abactor,* a useful word for all those who have ever tried to dig up their ancestors without using a shovel. Everyone dreams of finding a cattle rustler hanging from a branch of the family tree—and that's exactly what an abactor is: a cattle rustler. And *abaction* is "the stealing of a number of cattle at one time." Modern-day abactors perpetrate their dastardly deeds with the aid of huge tractor-trailer rigs (abactor tractors?) into which they herd dozens of bellowing steers at a time.

Except for those who are simply rustling up their next meal, most abactors today are in it for the money. We might even say they have a *pecuniary* interest in cattle (from Latin: *pecunia*—money). And not surprisingly, *pecunia* comes from *pecus,* the Latin word for cattle.

4 alphomeg

These docile beasts have been used as a yardstick—or meterstick—of wealth from ancient times to the present day. In his fascinating book on Africa, *No Room in the Ark,* Alan Moorehead writes: "According to the late Professor C. G. Seligman, an authority on the subject, it is impossible to exaggerate the importance of cattle to [the Karamojong tribe]. Cattle, he says, 'are so important that if an adjective stands by itself the noun it qualifies is always understood to be "cow".' "

I soon left *abactor* far behind as page after page passed before my dazzled eyes in daily succession. Exactly 1205 days later and right on schedule, I reached *zyxomma*—"a dragon-fly with large eyes and narrow head, found in India." Two days later, I coined *alphomeg.*

A famous Canadian alphomeg is Charles Templeton—broadcaster, journalist, and author of the bestselling novel, *Act of God.* As a young man, Templeton studied a page of the dictionary every night.

If you quail, shudder, wince, or cringe at the thought of spending months, or even *years,* reading a dictionary from cover to cover, cheer up! You can gallop through the pages of *Brave New Words* in just one evening.

andré

(ŏn-drā) noun.
The act of calling upon someone without forewarning, often to provide a pleasant surprise.
(eponym based on *André* Michael Cyr—see below)
Coined by Mark Fairclough, Ottawa, Ontario.

In explaining how this new word began, Fairclough writes:

> It happened like this: I was at André's house one day when he suggested we visit his girl friend. I asked if he had warned her and when he said "No," I replied: "So, we're going to do an andré on Louise."
> The word stuck and now has about 30 to 50 users in Ottawa and its use is growing.
> As you can see, the word is the name of a person. The act typifies his character.

André Michael Cyr now joins the English language as an eponym (a word based on someone's name). He'll not lack for company. Some of his eponymic cohorts include Captain Charles Boycott, the Earl of Cardigan, Nicolas Chauvin, the Earl of Chesterfield, Dr. Joseph Guillotin, Levi Strauss, Charles Mackintosh, Jean Nicot, Samuel Plimsoll, George Pullman, General Ambrose E. Burnside (who wore sideburns), and William A. Spooner.

For every person who becomes an eponym, there must be thousands more who want to be but don't know how. For those who yearn for this special kind of immortality, here's a do-it-yourself kit for eponymiacs:

Gouge tenants with high rents: Charles Boycott was a retired British army officer working as a land agent in Ireland in 1880. So vigorously did he squeeze the poverty-stricken tenants for every last penny of rent that they launched efforts to cut off his food supply and otherwise inconvenience him. Boycott is gone now but his name lives on. Anyone for California grapes?

Be a bootlicker: Nicolas Chauvin was a soldier in Napoleon's army who heaped so much praise on his leader that even Napoleon himself was said to be embarrassed. After Napoleon was sent into exile, Chauvin continued his Napoleonic chauvinism with such unabated zeal that he became an object of ridicule. Today, a male chauvinist promotes his own sex with the same blind devotion that Chauvin applied to Napoleon.

Invent a painless way of killing people: In the days before the French Revolution, executions were sometimes very sloppy, especially if the executioner showed up drunk. If he missed on the first swing, he just had to keep hacking away till the foul deed was done. In his search for a more humane way of killing people, Dr. Joseph Guillotin (1738-1814) invented—you guessed it!—the guillotine.

Start a new fad: Jean Nicot was the French ambassador at Lisbon in 1560. He planted some tobacco seeds he had been given by Portuguese sailors who had visited America; he also sent home tobacco to Catherine de Medicis, Queen of France. It wasn't long before millions of lungs were filled with nicotine. The fight for and against the "foul weed" has raged from that day to this.

Raise hell about safety at sea: For over a hundred years the North Atlantic was a graveyard for unfortunate souls who perished in "coffin ships"—heavily insured but dangerously overloaded vessels that would go down with all hands in the middle of a gale. Samuel Plimsoll, a British Member of Parliament, put a stop to this in 1876 when he rammed his reform legislation through Parliament. Henceforth, all ships were required to have Plimsoll lines (or maximum load lines) painted on the hull.

At least one fellow stumbled into the dictionary by accident. He was Reverend William Spooner (1844-1930), warden of New College, Oxford, and he had an unusual flair for hilarious verbal accidents. He reportedly wrapped up a marriage ceremony one day by saying to the groom, "Son, it is now kisstomary to cuss the bride." And to a young man who had wasted an entire term at school, Spooner said, "Sir, you have tasted your worm."

As *Toronto Star* columnist Robert Fulford points out, Spooner "became famous wherever an original form of eccentricity was appreciated. He enjoyed his curious reputation, and before he died he saw *spoonerism* appear in the Oxford English Dictionary."

If you still haven't figured out how to get *your* name into the dictionary, take a tip from Warren Beasley, operator of the miniature Centreville Golf and Country Club on Centre Island, just offshore from downtown Toronto. According to Toronto *Globe and Mail* columnist Dick Beddoes: "The miniature meadow is measured in beasles, a standard named after Warren Beasley, operator of the amusement park on Centre Island. A beasle equals one-tenth of a foot and metric be damned."

While you wait for Oxford or Webster to discover you, you can while away the hours playing with your surname—turning it into a verb, an adjective, an expletive, or whatever. Turn to *sherkquacious* to see how it's done.

baldephobia

(bŏl-dĕ-FŌ-bē-ă) noun.
The fear of going bald.
(Middle English: *balled*—bald; Greek: *phobia*—fear)
Coined by Marilyn Finkler, Toronto, Ontario.

Baldephobia is nothing new. Julius Caesar combed his hair forward to try to turn the tide of his hairy retreat. And another Roman named Pliny recommended sea horse ashes in honeyed vinegar as a cure for baldness. This concoction also supposedly cured hot flashes, skin eruptions, and the bite of a mad dog.

If you have a head full of healthy hair, don't feel too smug. Baldness (we have nudity, why not *baldity*?) can creep up on you faster than you can say, "Hair today, gone tomorrow." Just remember the words of the panic-stricken baldephobe: "Doctor, my hairline isn't just receding. It's evacuating!"

Not only can baldness be distressing, it can be downright dangerous as well. According to Colin Fletcher, in *Marvels and Mysteries of Our Animal World,* "In some parts of the world, eagles are reported to crack turtles by dropping them from a height. A Greek legend holds that the poet and dramatist Aeschylus was killed by a turtle-carrying eagle that mistook his bald head for a rock."

Our feathered friends usually don't worry about going bald. (When was the last time you saw a bird wearing a toupé?) Even the bald eagle really isn't bald at all but simply has a topnotch of white feathers. This was the bird chosen by Congress in 1782 for the Great Seal of the United States. Rejected was Benjamin Franklin's proposal that the turkey gobbler be adopted as the national emblem of the fledgling republic.

If old Ben had had his way, the first manned landing on the moon—July 20, 1969—would have followed a different script. Instead of hearing "Tranquillity Base. The *Eagle* has landed," we would have heard, "Tranquillity Base. The *Turkey* has landed."

baldephobia 9

bicyclivore

(bī-SĬK-lĭ-vōr) noun.
A person who eats bicycles.
(Latin: *bi*—two; Greek: *kuklos*—a wheel; Latin: *vorax*—greedy to devour)
Coined by the author.

The following story appeared in *The Toronto Star* on Monday April 4, 1977:

Waiter! One Bike Well Done

(Evry, France—Reuter) Frenchman Michel Lolito last night finished eating a bicycle, a feat that took him two weeks of solid chewing.

Lolito, better known as Mr. Mangetout (eat-all), was participating in the 11th Festival of Silly Records, a freakish annual circus.

bicyclivore

He said the easiest part was the chain because its coating of grease helped it slide down more easily than, say, the tires. He has now set his eyes—and teeth—on eating a car.

Carnivores eat meat, herbivores eat plants, and omnivores eat almost anything (the cockroach, if hungry enough, will eat its own skin after moulting). But Lolito is clearly in a class all by himself. He's a *bicyclivore!*

And if he gets around to chomping on a car, he'll be a full-fledged *vehiclivore*. The accent falls on the second syllable (vē-HĬK-lĭ-vōr) because the fuel in the gas tank could give him the hiccups.

bioopsy

(bī-ŌOP-sē) noun.
A biopsy performed on living tissue after it has been accidentally (oops!) dropped on the floor. In other words, a sloppy biopsy.
(Greek: *bios*—life; *opsis*—sight; *oops!*)
Coined by the author.

Bioopsy is a very handy word if you happen to be a clumsy lab technician. Each time you drop a piece of living tissue to the floor, you'll be picking up another load of microscopic hitchhikers. If you're *really* clumsy in the lab, you might end up performing a bioop-oop-oop-oopsy.

Surprisingly enough, *oops!* is missing from many regular dictionaries ("Oops! We forgot to put it in."). Not even the 12-volume *Oxford English Dictionary* (OED) stoops to include *oops!*—which is ironic because if we capitalize OOPS, then drop the S and chop the top off the second O, we end up with OUP, the initials of Oxford University Press, which publishes the OED.

As these very words are being written (June 1978), the Oxford University Press is in the throes of celebrating its five hundredth anniversary. Its first book appeared back in 1478 and over the

following centuries the Oxford press has tasted both feast and famine. In the Toronto *Globe and Mail,* William French writes: "The Bible boom in the nineteenth century helped the Oxford press establish a solid financial base. It brought prosperity to certain farmers, too; at the peak of the boom, the skins of 100,000 goats per year were used in the covers. The skin of an average goat covered 10 bibles."

On the famine side of the ledger we find Wilkin's *Coptic Gospels,* published in 1716 in a 500-copy edition. Not exactly a best seller, the last copy was snapped up in 1907, nearly 200 years later. And book lovers stayed away in droves when *Certain Variations in the Vocal Organs of the Passeres (That Have Hitherto Escaped Notice)* went on sale. Despite a plug from Charles Darwin himself, only 21 copies were sold in 25 years.

Happy birthday, OUP! And catch up to Webster by putting *oops!* in your next edition.

bladderclock

(BLĂD-ĕr-klŏk) noun.
The urinary bladder when used as an alarm clock.
(Old English: *blaedre*—a blister; French: *cloche*—a bell)
Coined by the author.

The *bladderclock* is the answer to your prayers if you've ever slept right through the ringing of your alarm clock or telephone wake-up service. And it doesn't cost you a cent because you've already got one—supplied free of charge by Mother Nature!

All you have to do is drink just enough water before going to bed at night to guarantee being awakened in the morning by the need to urinate. And if the need to urinate doesn't wake you up, you'll wet the bed and *that* will wake you up.

Either way, your sleep is shattered.

blupper

(BLŬP-ŭr) noun.
A single daily meal in place of breakfast, lunch, and supper.
(*breakfast* from Old English: *brecan*—to break; *faestan*—to fast; *lunch* possibly from Spanish: *lonja*—slice; *supper* from French: *souper*—to sup)
Coined and used regularly by Sybil and Burton Cowitz, Downsview, Ontario.

Blupper is the perfect word for anyone who wants to lose weight fast: "Now that I'm on a diet, I'm down to only one meal a day: blupper!"
  And if you stick to your daily blupper, you will soon lose all your excess blubber.
  Here's how to make Leonardo da Vinci roll over in his grave: When you get your weight down to where you want it, have someone paint your picture at the blupper-table the day before you go back to three squares a day. Then hang it on the wall and call it *The Last Blupper*.
  As a word, *blupper* can be used as both noun and verb. When you're eating dinner, you're dining. And when you're eating blupper, you're blupping! But when during the day should you blup? That's entirely up to you. Bluppertime is anytime.

  See also: *brunner* and *lupper*.

brunner

(BRŬN-ĕr) noun.
A single daily meal in place of breakfast, lunch, and dinner. (*breakfast* from Old English: *brecan*—to break; *faestan*—to fast; *lunch* possibly from Spanish: *lonja*—slice; *dinner* from French: *dîner*—to dine)
Coined jointly by Donald Cudmore of Halifax, Nova Scotia, and Stephen Skoutajan of Toronto, Ontario, while Cudmore was visiting Skoutajan.

Brunner was coined in Toronto during the 1978 Christmas holidays. Hence the first brunner was a Yule Brunner (with apologies to Yul Brynner). Cudmore and Skoutajan (who recommend 2:30 P.M. as the ideal brunnertime) see their new word performing many useful and varied functions: A *brunnerer* is a person who eats brunner every day by choice. In other words, instead of eating three square meals a day, he eats one big rectangular meal. A *brunneree*, on the other hand, is someone whose doctor has prescribed a single daily meal as a means of losing weight. A *brunnic* is a brunner eaten as a picnic ("Let's go on a brunnic!"). "*Brunner-up!*" (formerly "Runner-up!") describes anyone placing second in an all-day pie-eating contest. A *brunnerteria* is a cafeteria which serves all meals at all hours. If U.S. comedian David Brenner ever opens an all-night restaurant, he can call it *Brenner's Brunnery*. And if your car battery goes dead while you're eating brunner at Brenner's drive-in restaurant, you can call yourself a *brunnererer..er....er......er........*

But wait! *Brave New Words* already contains *blupper*, which has exactly the same meaning as brunner. Surely there isn't room in this dictionary for both these new words. One of them will have to be thrown out. But which one?

As luck would have it, we can save both these words from linguistic oblivion. Blupper can be re-defined as a *hot* single daily meal (when the gravy starts bubbling on the stove, it goes *blup-blup-blup-blup*). Brunner, on the other hand, can be served cold (br-r-r-r). And if you eat it with the thermostat turned down, you could call it *br-r-r-runner.*

Br-r-r-runner also comes in handy for describing someone who likes to go jogging in sub-zero weather. For those who like to run and brun in all kinds of weather, be sure to read *The Complete Book of Brunning* by James Fixxameal.

As you can see, it's only a matter of time before brunner breaches the walls of official usage and takes its rightful place in standard English dictionaries. When it does, it will be only three or four entries below *brummer*, which the *Webster Universal Dictionary* defines as: "A large insect of South Africa, akin to the house-fly, which lives on the larva of locusts." If the day ever comes when a shortage of food forces us to eat insects, a brunner full of brummer would be a real "bummer."

bubbliophile

(BŬB-lē-ō-fīl) noun.
A lover of champagne.
(Middle English: *bobelen*—bubble; Greek: *philos*—loving)
Coined by Michael Bolitho, Toronto, Ontario.

By the time you read this page, *Brave New Words* will be on sale in bookstores throughout North America. And that means *bubbliophile* will be at the beck and call of over 250 million people. But will they use this new word only in reference to champagne? Some people might extend the meaning to include a lover of all carbonated drinks. Others might apply it to someone who likes to take bubble baths. *Bubbliophile* might even extend its linguistic grasp to include someone who likes to stand on the rim of volcanoes to watch the boiling lava bubbling up from the innards of the earth.

One such watcher of bubbling lava might be Michael Bolitho himself, coiner of *bubbliophile*. His very surname—Bolitho—appears to be volcanic in origin. The Greek root for stone is *lithos* (as in *Paleolithic* or Old Stone Age) and if the *bo* in his name is a contraction of the Middle English *bobelen* (bubble), then his name is literally Michael Bubblestone. And stones that contain air bubbles are known as pumice-stones. These are formed high in the air from lava ejected from volcanoes. Tons of pumice-stone fell upon the ancient Roman city of Pompeii when Mount Vesuvius erupted on August 24, 79 A.D.

But Vesuvius is not the only volcano in Italy. Stromboli and Etna are there as well, and all three have been vividly described by Gordon Gaskill in a *Reader's Digest* article (October 1973) salaciously entitled "Italy's Three Red-Hot Sisters." Stromboli, unlike the other two, rises out of the waters of the Tyrrhenian Sea and is *always* active—smoking by day and glowing by night. Ancient Greeks called her the "Lighthouse of the Mediterranean."

Seventy miles south of Stromboli is Etna, the highest mountain on the island of Sicily. This volcano was the home of Vulcan, the ancient Roman god of fire and metallurgy whose name has given us the word *volcano*.

His wife's name ended up in the dictionary too, for he was married to Venus, the goddess of love, who gave the English language *venereal disease*. We don't know if Venus gave the disease to her husband but we do know she had a torrid love affair with Mars, the red-hot Roman god of war. Maybe this is why Vulcan set up his forge on Mount Etna and began fashioning thunderbolts for Jupiter— Venus was no longer around to keep him warm. At any rate, Vulcan came to be known as the special patron of cuckolds. We could even call him the king of cuckoldom.

Of the three red-hot volcanic sisters, Vesuvius is by far the best known. Her lava is extra thick and gets clogged in her throat like the cork in a bottle of champagne. When the pressure inside builds up to the breaking point, the "cork" shoots out and the mountain spews the fires of hell into the sky.

A similar eruption, but on a smaller scale, takes place every New Year's Eve when partygoers pop the cork on bottles of champagne. The true bubbliophile will not wish to waste any of this bubbly wine if he can possibly help it. In "Let's Get Our Kicks From Champagne" (*The City* magazine of the *Toronto Star,* December 24, 1978), magazine editor Bill MacVicar tells us how to do it: "Opening a bottle of champagne is a ticklish business—the trick is to hold the bottle at a 45-degree angle, and *slowly* twist the *bottle* away from the cork (a white towel folded over the neck, with about an inch of slack, is an almost foolproof precaution). This tip is never more useful than at 11:59 on New Year's Eve, as the cork goes off with the downbeat of the band leader's baton."

bugicide

(BŬG-ĭ-sīd) noun.
The killing of insects by non-chemical means.
(*bug*—origin obscure; *cide* from Latin: *caedere*—to kill)
Coined by the author.

Bugicide should not be confused with insecticide which *The Webster Universal Dictionary* defines as: "The act of killing insect pests by spraying, dusting, or gas-poisoning; chemical preparation for the destruction of noxious insects." By contrast, *bugicide* is cheaper, simpler, and faster. You can get rid of pesky bugs by stomping them underfoot, mashing them with a flyswatter, or slamming a book shut when they land on an open page.

bus-lag

(BŬS-lăg) noun.
The feeling you get when you miss your cross-country bus but your luggage does not.
(*bus* from Latin: *omnibus*—for all; Celtic: *lag*—lag)
Coined by Michael Perkins, Toronto, Ontario.

Lots of people prefer to take the bus and leave their car at home—and some people who ride the bus prefer to do without a car altogether. Dave Robertson of Toronto says, for example, "Why should I spend over five thousand dollars on a car when I can ride around town in a $150,000 bus?"

cabloop

(kăb-LOOP) verb.
To drive a taxicab by a roundabout route to raise the fare. "Driver! I refuse to pay for all this cablooping!"
(taxi*cab* from French: *taximetre*—a metre for tax or charge; *loop* probably from Irish: *lub*—a bend)
Coined by Robert Warren, Toronto, Ontario.

Taxicabs have been around for a long time. Back in the days of Julius Caesar you could flag down a chariot and go for a fast gallop along the Appian Way or a leisurely clippety-clop around the Seven Hills of Rome. When your ride was over, the charioteer told you to cough up the fare.

But how did he know how much to charge you?

Some chariots had a tin can full of pebbles mounted near the axle. As the axle turned, a disc at the bottom of the can rotated and allowed a pebble to fall through a hole into another can below. By counting the number of pebbles that had fallen through, the driver could calculate the fare. The Latin word for *pebble* is *calculus,* and that's where our word *calculate* comes from.

Some cab drivers in Roman times did very well for themselves, especially those who plied their trade in Pompeii. In *Lost Cities and Vanished Civilizations* Robert Silverberg takes us to that ancient Roman city: "Arriving at Pompeii today, you leave your car outside and enter through an age-old gate . . . . The streets are narrow and deeply rutted with the tracks of chariot wheels. Only special narrow Pompeiian chariots could travel inside the town. Travelers from outside were obliged to change vehicles when they reached the walls of the city. This provided a profitable monopoly for the Pompeiian equivalent of cab drivers, 20 centuries ago!"

If a penny-pinching visitor tried to sneak his own chariot into the city, he wouldn't get past the first intersection: "At each intersection, blocks of stone . . . are mounted in the roadway, so designed that chariot wheels could pass on either side of them. 'Those are steppingstones for the people of Pompeii,' your guide tells you. Pompeii had no sewers, and during heavy rainfalls the streets were flooded with many inches of water. The Pompeiians could keep their feet dry by walking on those stones."

The taxi business—and everthing else—in Pompeii came to an abrupt end on August 24, 79 A.D., when Mount Vesuvius erupted nearby and buried the city under a blanket of pumice and volcanic ash. And thus the city slept for 17 centuries—until canal diggers accidentally stumbled upon it in 1748. As you might expect, they found no taxicabs with the meter still running.

Canuckophile

(kă-NŬK-ō-fĭl) noun.
A person who loves Canada and/or Canadians.
(*Canuck* + Greek: *philos*—loving)
Coined by the author.

Many Americans could describe themselves as incurable *Canuckophiles*, especially those with fond memories of vacations spent in the land of beaver, moose, and the Royal Canadian Mounted Police. If you are, at this very moment, planning to visit Canada for the first time, *take fair warning:* When you get back home, a sudden attack of Canuckophilia could strike you at any time—and the only effective cure is a return visit.

According to Canadian poet John Robert Colombo, the word *Canuck* ("a light-hearted reference to a Canadian") first appeared in print in 1849. But despite a lifespan of over 125 years, this term is not widely known in the United States. Prompted by a query from one of his readers, *New York Times* columnist William Safire wrote to Canadian Prime Minister Pierre Trudeau on December 29, 1976, asking his opinion of the current meaning and usage of Canuck. According to Trudeau,

> As with all slang, and especially that of nationality, the implications of the word vary a great deal according to the context and intent of the speaker or writer. Opinion also varies as to who exactly is designated by the word Canuck.
>
> Many Canadians feel it refers to all Canadians, some believe it is eastern Canadians, others that it is French Canadians, while the majority have rarely heard it used in any context.
>
> Although much less widely used than the word "Yankee," its connotations have more or less the same range. We have a hockey team called the Vancouver Canucks, as you have a baseball team called the New York Yankees.
>
> "Johnny Canuck" was the personification of an English Canadian war hero in a comic strip. The Yankee of "I'm a Yankee Doodle Dandy . . ." is not the same as "Yankee, Go Home." Thus you can see that the question is not easily

answered. Whether or not you committed an ethnic slur would depend entirely on the way the word was used. . . .

Pierre Trudeau has not yet expressed an opinion on Canuckophile, but the English language will be lacking a certain something if this word goes unrecognized. Open any dictionary worth its weight in printer's ink and you can find *Anglophile, Francophile,* and *Russophile* for people who love England or France or Russia. And in *The Barnhart Dictionary of New English Since 1963,* you can find *Yankeephile* for those who love the United States.

Yankee, by the way, has more than one meaning. *The Heritage Illustrated Dictionary* supplies three definitions: 1) a native or inhabitant of New England; 2) a native or inhabitant of a northern state; especially a Union soldier during the Civil War; 3) a native or inhabitant of the United States.

During the Civil War, southerners spoke of Yankees as if they were foreigners (as indeed they were if you belonged to the Confederacy). When the northern armies were advancing on Atlanta in *Gone With The Wind,* Scarlett O'Hara's Aunt Pittypat cried, "Yankees in Georgia! How did they ever get in?"

ceilopittura

(sĕ-lō-pĭ-TŪR-ă) noun.
A painting done directly on a ceiling.
(*ceiling* + Italian: *pittura*—painting)
Coined by John Rutherford, Scarborough, Ontario.

In defence of *ceilopittura,* Rutherford points out:

> A *mural* is a painting done directly on a wall but there is no word in the English language that I know of that means "a painting done directly on a ceiling." Creating a word would save us from such misunderstandings as: *Question:* When you were in Rome, did you see the Sistine Chapel ceiling? *Answer:* No. When I was there it had already been covered with paint. If the questioner had said, "Did you see Michelangelo's *ceilopittura?*", no misunderstanding could have occurred. Then too, Michelangelo could have been referred to as a *ceilopitturalist.*

And another question: Why did Michelangelo take *four years to* paint the Sistine Chapel ceiling? *Answer:* Because he used a brush instead of a roller.

Calling all word coiners! We now have ceilings and walls covered with paint, but still no word for a painting done directly on the floor. If you paint your basement floor all the colours of the rainbow, you'll certainly want a very special word to describe your handiwork. *Mosaic* won't do because a mosaic is a patchwork of coloured stones, not a painting.

If you come up with a word that will cover an artistically painted floor, fill out the word card at the back of this book and pop it into the nearest mail box. Your word (and your name!) could hit the next edition of *Brave New Words.*

connoizer

(kŏ-NOY-zĕr) noun.
A person who *pretends* to be a connoisseur of the fine arts.
(based on how a connoizer might mispronounce "connoisseur")
Coined by, but not descriptive of, Paul Dodington, Port Carling, Ontario.

In *Impressions of America* Oscar Wilde (1856-1900) describes a connoizer in the old West: "So infinitesimal did I find the knowledge of Art, west of the Rocky Mountains, that an art patron—one who in his day had been a miner—actually sued the railroad company for damages because the plaster cast of Venus de Milo, which he had imported from Paris, had been delivered minus the arms. And, what is more surprising still, he gained his case and the damages."

connoizer

This hassle could have been avoided if our connoizerly art patron had ordered the statue through an illustrated Sears and Roebuck catalogue. On the other hand, there could still be a problem. He might think the arms had to be ordered separately.

The statue of Venus de Milo was found (minus arms, of course) in 1820 on the island of Melos in the Aegean Sea. In his monumental classic, *The Life of Greece,* Will Durant describes this armless wonder as "the most famous statue in the Western world." It was chiselled by an unknown chiseller (oops! . . . *sculptor*) to glorify Venus, the goddess of love. The Romans called her Venus but to the Greeks she was known as Aphrodite (ă-frō-DIGHT-ē).

Although Venus no doubt had regular medical check-ups on Mount Olympus, her name has been repeatedly linked with venereal disease. And no wonder. If we check the etymology of *venereal,* we find the Latin root to be none other than *Venus, Veneris,* the goddess of love.

Venus also pops up in another part of your dictionary—under *aphrodisiac,* which comes from her Greek name, Aphrodite. According to *The Reader's Encyclopedia,* "she wore a magic girdle which enabled its wearer to arouse love in others." Try ordering *that* through a mail-order catalogue.

Incidentally, unbeknownst to the modern world, Aphrodite had a twin sister in the lingerie business. Her name was Aphronite (ă-frō-NIGHT-ē) and she sold her wares (her *underwares*) from a little shop in the crotch of an olive tree on the outskirts of Athens. Some of her biggest customers were the gods and goddesses who lived on Mount Olympus. For years she supplied Zeus with all his jockey shorts.

So far, no statue of Aphronite has ever been found. If some lucky archaeologist one day digs her up, we'll recognize her immediately. She was the only Greek goddess who wore her hair in an Aphro.

covivant

(kō-vē-VŎNGH) noun. Rhymes with *bon vivant*.
An unmarried person who is living on intimate terms with a member of the opposite sex. "Mother and Dad, I'd like you to meet Debbie, my covivant."
(Latin: *co*—together; *vivere*—to live)
Coined by Shirley Yamada, Toronto, Ontario.

For years now, the English language has been begging—nay, *screaming!*—for just such a word. According to Sidney Katz of *The Toronto Star:*

> The question is one that is confronting more and more parents in an era of sexual liberation: How to refer to—or for that matter, introduce—their son's female roommate or their daughter's live-in boy friend.
>
> Some skirt the problem by using such words as "fiancée," "cohab," "inamorata," "significant other," or simply "boy friend" and "girl friend." None of these terms, however, precisely connotes the nature and status of the relationship.*

Co-hab probably comes closest because it's a contraction of *cohabit:* "to live together in a sexual relationship when not legally married" (Heritage Dictionary). And sociologists have used the term *cohabitation* for some time now to refer to marriageless unions. But *co-hab* has yet to achieve universal acceptance. Perhaps it sounds too clinical—or too temporary. And it certainly sounds out of place on a moonlit night: "Oh, Darling, will you be . . . I mean, would you like to be . . . my *co-hab?*"

To save this tender scene, *covivant* comes rushing to the rescue. With its impeccable Latin credentials and its francophonic pronunciation, it gives your conversation just the right dash of romantic delicacy and continental sophistication. As Shirley Yamada herself points out, "The word is even bilingual. What more could you want?"

After talking about Shirley's new word on a Toronto radio pro-

*From *"What has 9 letters, starts with G, and sleeps with your son?"* by Sidney Katz. *The Toronto Star,* May 21, 1977. The title of Katz' article is based on *grynnflnk* (GRĬN-flĭnk), a word coined by two Minneapolis mothers of single children living with a sexual partner. These two mothers needed a word to refer to their offsprings' mate. They took the letters left over after a game of Scrabble and came up with *grynnflnk*.

30 covivant

gramme, I received the following letter from Mrs. Marilyn Ciantar of Kitchener, Ontario:

> Dear Mr. Sherk:
>
> I was listening to you speak on "Our Toronto" at noon today, and would like to thank you for an answer to a problem I have had for a while now. We have friends who are living together, not married, and none of us ever knew how to introduce them. The word "covivant" is a lovely sounding word, and really does fit the situation perfectly.
>
> Thanks for your help!

crotchocrat

(KRŎCH-ō-krăt) noun.
A person who encourages a minority group to increase its political power by raising large families.
(etymology of *crotch* uncertain; *crat* from Greek: *kratein*—to rule) Coined by the author.

The coining of *crotchocrat* was inspired by a news item in *The Toronto Star* on March 19, 1977:

> **Montreal (CP)**—English-speaking Quebeckers can ensure the survival of their language by making love, Quebec Premier Rene Levesque said last night.
> Quebec's English-speaking minority should take its own "revenge of the cradles" on the French-speaking majority by raising large families, he told reporters.
> He said the future "growth" of English in Quebec under his government's language charter . . . is "up to the power of your loins."
> "Revenge of the cradles" was the phrase used to describe the French-Canadians' birth rate that enabled their language and culture to survive the British conquest of New France in 1759.

When I sat down to coin a word for what Levesque was advocating, I first thought of *loinocrat* (". . . it's up to the power of your loins"), but I quickly dismissed it because *loinocrat* sounds like a militant member of a butchers' union. I also rejected *groinocrat* on the grounds that *groin* is often mentioned in the same breath as *hernia*. And then *crotchocrat* sprang to mind! It's the perfect word for at least two reasons: 1) It's a pleasure to pronounce because it's full of alliteration; 2) It means what it says it means. Not all words can make that claim. Hernia applies to both men and women but you'd think a man's hernia would be a *hisnia*.

Premier Levesque has clearly flung a challenge at the reproductive capacity of English-speaking Quebeckers. Will their loins rise to the challenge? It's still too early to tell—but one thing is certain. They should *not*, as the saying goes, gird up their loins for the struggle ahead because girded loins will only make their task more difficult.

32 crotchocrat

For those who want large families, ungirded loins are a must.

In no time at all, political experts will begin to study crotchocratic movements around the world. In doing so, they will quickly stumble upon a basic truth: a crotchocracy can flourish only in a democracy (in which more voters = more power). In a country like Russia, the whole concept of majority rule is meaningless. If, for example, the Byelorussians start breeding like rabbits, they still won't have any more clout in the Kremlin. So if you're waiting for crotchocrat to appear in a Russian dictionary (*crotchocratnik?*), you'll have a long wait.

cybrow

(SĪ-brow) noun.
A person whose eyebrows are joined together.
(*cy* from *Cyclopes*, a race of one-eyed giants in ancient Greek mythology; Old English *brú*—brow)
Coined by Matthew Trowel, Toronto, Ontario.

Do you know any *cybrows*?
They're difficult to find because many of them pluck out the hairs that grow between their eyebrows. This practice is to be deplored. It's not only unnatural, it's uncomfortable too. The purpose of eyebrows is to keep drops of perspiration from rolling off your forehead and into your eyes. But without a hairy rampart above your nose, salty rivulets of sweat will roll down either side of your nose and into your mouth. Ugh!

A sweaty cybrow, however, never has this problem. His or her one big brow diverts the flow of moisture to the sides of the face where it then rolls down the cheeks, down the neck, onto the torso and from there ends up who knows where. Two heads may be better than one, but one big eyebrow is better than two. And if the "cybrow look" ever becomes popular, wig manufacturers could make a real killing by selling tiny tufts of hair to stick on your face just above the bridge of your nose.

The first cybrows to make their mark in history were of course the Cyclopes, that race of one-eyed giants who lived in the pages of ancient Greek literature. The most famous of these monocular monsters was a fellow named Polyphemus who lived in a cave and herded sheep for a living. He came home one day to discover the Greek hero Odysseus and his men had stopped in on their way home from the Trojan Wars and were helping themselves to his food. He snatched up two of them, dashed their brains out against a rock, and devoured them for dinner. The next day at breakfast he ate two more, then another two at lunch.

Only the quick thinking of Odysseus saved the rest of them from the same fate. He plied the giant with wine till he fell fast asleep. Then Odysseus and his men sharpened a huge tree trunk (which just happened to be lying around in the cave) and drove it into the sleeping giant's eye. Writhing in sudden agony, Polyphemus began screaming for his neighbouring Cyclopes to come running to his rescue. But none of them came because Odysseus had cunningly told Polyphemus that his name was No One and the now-blinded giant was bellowing, "Help! Help! No One is trying to kill me!"

If Polyphemus were alive today with his sight restored, he would probably be driving around in a 1948 Tucker automobile. In addition to its two front headlights, the Tucker had a "cyclopean" headlight mounted in the middle which turned with the steering wheel to help the driver see around corners. The designer and builder, Preston Tucker, wanted the front fenders to turn as well but his engineers convinced him it was impractical.

Only about 50 of these cars were built in postwar Detroit before the company collapsed. The Tucker is now a highly prized collector's item. So if you have one, Polyphemus, hang onto it. The price can only go up!

dactylometry

(dăk-tĭl-ŎM-ĕ-trē) noun.
Measurement by hand span or finger thickness. "Bartender! I want a shot of whiskey two fingers high!"
(Greek: *daktulos*—finger; *metron*—measure)
Coined by Alex Logothetopoulos, Toronto, Ontario.

Do you find yourself caught in the middle of the metric conversion, wondering which way to go? You were born in pounds and ounces, raised on quarts of milk, and driven around in miles per gallon. Now you're being thrust against your will into a bewildering world of litres, kilometres, and grams—right?
 Well, cheer up! You don't have to go metric or stay the way you are. Now there's a third possibility: you can measure length, weight, and volume according to your own personal bodily measurements! Just think, a completely personalized measuring system that you carry around with you—automatically—wherever you go. Ordering a shot of whiskey two fingers high (*your* fingers) is simply one of the more obvious applications.
 For measuring weight, all you have to do is carry a spring-loaded teeter-totter with you. By standing on one end, you can weigh everything as a percentage of your own weight.
 For measuring volume, your *whole* body may be too big and unwieldy. Instead, why not use your head? Carry a balloon with you which, when fully blown up, is the exact volume of your head. Imagine how useful this would be in a supermarket when you're shopping for a *head* of lettuce or a *head* of cabbage. You've always wondered, "Whose head?" Now you can tell the store clerk it's *your* head. And if you're a fathead, you might get a discount.
 Other parts of the body can be pressed into service as well, especially if you're shopping for a *leg* of lamb or a *breast* of chicken.
 Since *dactylometry* applies only to hand span or finger thickness, we obviously need an all-embracing *full-bodied* word, of which *dactylometry* is only a part. May I suggest *fleshometrics? Flesh* can be used to mean *body* as in: "The spirit is willing but the flesh is weak." If you use your body or parts thereof to measure things, you can now call yourself a *fleshometrist* (flĕsh-ŎM-ĕ-trĭst).
 And as an added bonus, the *flesh* in *fleshometrics* adds a certain spicy raciness to an otherwise dull topic. Ahh! The pleasures of the flesh. . . .

dek

(dĕk) noun.
A group of 10.
(Greek: *deka*—ten)
Coined by John Rutherford, Scarborough, Ontario.

In defence of this new word, Rutherford writes, "Now that we are going metric, may I suggest the word *dek* (a group of ten) to replace the word *dozen*. A *dollar a dek* has a nice ring, and *twenty* would become a *double dekker*." If Rutherford has his way, you might soon be buying a dek of eggs and a 10-pack of pop. But be careful. If you ask for a deck of cards, you might end up with only 10 instead of 52.

Zealous converts to the metric system will undoubtedly meet their biggest challenge when they grapple with our calendar which has—alas!—12 months instead of 10. The word *month* comes from the Old English word *mona* (moon) and our 12-month calendar is based on the fact that the moon circles the earth slightly over 12 times a year. If we could figure out some way of pushing the moon further away from the earth—into a bigger orbit at a slower speed—we would then have a moon that circled the earth *exactly 10 times a year!* Ten-month calendars could then be rushed into production.

A quick glance at the last four months of our present calendar is enough to make the hearts of metric lovers leap for joy. September, October, November, and December contain the numbers *seven* (*sept*), *eight* (*octo*), *nine* (*novem*), and *ten* (*decem*). But these four months occupy the ninth, tenth, eleventh, and twelfth positions on our calendar. Why this discrepancy?

The answer can be found in the old Roman calendar which began each new year in March—hence, September *was* the seventh month, October the eighth, and so on. In 153 B.C., January became the first month—but the months from September to December still retained their original names.

The Roman calendar was overhauled again in 46 B.C. when Julius Caesar introduced the Julian calendar (he borrowed it from Egypt, where the charms of Cleopatra made it difficult for him to keep track of the time). Because the old Roman calendar of 355 days was hopelessly out of date, Caesar changed the length of the year to 365 days, with an extra day added every four years. Because this calendar was inaccurate by 11 minutes and 14 seconds per year, it was over a week behind by 1582 when Pope Gregory XIII introduced a modified version known as the Gregorian calendar (the one we follow today).

In case future generations might forget the big splash Julius Caesar made in ancient Rome, Quintilis (the month of his birth) was renamed *July* in his honour. Not to be outdone, his nephew Octavius (who became the Emperor Augustus) had *his* birth month, Sextilis (from Latin: *sexa*—six), renamed *August*.

Food for thought: If you were born in May (nine months after August), you owe your life to the sex in Sextilis.

dentiphobia

(děn-tĭ-FŌ-bē-ă) noun.
The fear of going to the dentist.
(Latin: *dens*—tooth; Greek: *phobia*—fear)
Coined by Ilze Villers, Toronto, Ontario.

Dentiphobia is a fear that's fading fast. Thanks to fluoride, more and more youngsters can say, "Look, Ma! No cavities!"

But where does all this leave the dentists? According to Phil McCavity, a tooth-puller in Swollen Gums, Saskatchewan, dentists may someday have to resort to house calls to maintain their present-day volume of business. McCavity even foresees the day when the streets will be filled with radio-dispatched tooth trucks giving curb-side dental work.

Unemployed dentists might do well to consider a career in gardening. Instead of pulling teeth, they could pull weeds. And linguistically speaking, many front lawns have teeth growing on them. The word *dandelion* comes from the French *dent de lion* (tooth of lion) because the little pointed green leaves under the yellow top look like lions' teeth.

A word of warning: If your dentist suddenly starts whistling "The Yanks Are Coming" while he's checking your teeth, you'll soon be trading in your real teeth for a set of dentures. But don't feel too bad. In his book, *Clark Gable,* Rene Jordan reminds us that even the King of Hollywood himself had false teeth: "When MGM insisted that he replace his hopeless teeth with double plates, Douglas Fairbanks, Sr., heard of this savory piece of news. Then jealous of the rising Gable, Fairbanks asked women how they could love the man he called "the toothless wonder." Gable knew this and once startled Mrs. Cole Porter by removing his dentures in front of her, after she had praised his gleaming smile."

And now for a snappy one-liner from Milton Berle: "Sorry, folks! My tongue got caught in my eyeteeth and I couldn't see what I was saying."

doonic

(DOO-nĭk) noun.
The sound produced by bouncing a balloon with a string tied to your finger. Also useful as a verb. *Mother:* "Johnny, what are you doing?" *Johnny:* "I'm doonicking."
(onomatopoetic)
Coined by Ina Roelants, Duncan, British Columbia.

Some balloons are too big for *doonicking*. One such balloon carried two Frenchmen over Paris nearly two hundred years ago:

> The date was November 21, 1783; the place, the Bois de Boulogne in Paris. An excited crowd looked on as two French aristocrats, Jean-François Pilâtre de Rozier and the Marquis d'Arlandes, climbed into a tub-like circular "gallery" suspended below a huge linen bag inflated with hot air from a fire of straw. A natural historian by profession, Pilâtre de Rozier was the hero of the hour. When Louis XVI offered to supply two condemned prisoners to risk the perils of being hoisted aloft, the historian had exclaimed: "Shall vile criminals have the honour of first rising in the sky? I myself shall go!" ["The Challenge of the Sky." Royal Bank of Canada Monthly Letter, June 1978.]

Fourteen months later, two brave souls set out from Dover to cross the English Channel by balloon. While over the water, they lost so much altitude they threw nearly everything overboard, including most of the clothes they wore. This was the first air-strip in history. They finally came down—nearly naked—in the woods near Calais.

In June, 1785, the now-famous Pilâtre de Rozier decided to conquer the English Channel the other way—from France to England. He didn't make it. His balloon burst into flames at 3000 feet, giving him the dubious honour of being history's first fatality of flight.

According to "The Challenge of the Sky," two other milestones were reached that same year with "the first aerial hijacker, who jumped with sword drawn into the car beside a well-known French balloonist and demanded to be taken along (he was overpowered by the ground crew), and the first stunt flyer, who flew sitting astride a horse."

Duncday

(DŬNK-dā) noun.
A proposed new eighth day to be added to the end of every week.
(eponym based on Lloyd *Dunc*an)
Coined by Lloyd Duncan, Oakville, Ontario, who says, "We need an extra day at the end of each week to catch up on everything."

Lloyd Duncan is not the only one who has dreamed of having an eight-day week (with the eighth day a holiday, of course). Back in the 1960s the Beatles put this idea to music when they recorded their hit song, *Eight Days a Week*. But as far as I know, Lloyd Duncan is the first person in recorded history to actually give this extra day a name. And he exercised his word coiner's prerogative by naming the day after himself.

Right now, you're probably thinking: "Doggone it! Why didn't I think of that? I could have had *my* name in the dictionary!" Well, it's not too late. The last day of a *nine*-day week is still up for grabs.

Because Sunday is considered the first day of the week and Saturday the last, *Duncday* will have to be squeezed in right after Saturday. This will come as good news to all those who burn the candle at both ends every Saturday night.

Converting our calendar to eight-day weeks could, however, cause some problems. The last time our calendar was overhauled was back in 1751 when the British Parliament voted to replace the old Julian calendar with the more accurate Gregorian. The people of England went to bed on the evening of September 2 and woke up the next day to find it was September 14. Riots broke out in the rural parts of England as people ran through the streets shouting, "Give us back our eleven days!"

Our present calendar, the Gregorian, is still far from perfect. The International Fixed Calendar League wants to replace our present calendar of 12 months of varying length with a calendar of 13 equal periods per year. By doing so, each "month" would have 28 days and each date would always fall on the same day of the week. Payroll accountants and government statisticians would be eternally grateful if such a calendar were adopted. So would churches. With 53 Sundays in 1978 instead of 52, the bookkeeping required to keep

Duncday

track of the money on the collection plate was horrendous!

Under this new scheme, if you divide 13 into 365 ¼, you find one day left over (two days on a leap year). Because all the other days of the year would be permanently fastened to specific days of the week, this extra day would be floating around loose with no name. Taking my cue from Lloyd Duncan, I propose we call it *Sherkday*. We can change the spelling to *Shirkday* and declare it to be a fun-filled, carefree national holiday—a day, once a year, when we can shirk all our responsibilities.

And once every four years, we'll have two such holidays side by side. We should lump both those days together and call them *Doubleday*. That should make the publisher of this book very happy.

duodemilingual

(doo-ō-dĕ-mē-LĬNG-gwăl) adjective.
Knowing two languages and part of a third.
(Latin: *duo*—two; French: *demi*—half; Latin: *lingua*—a tongue)
Coined by Ray Nakamura, Toronto, Ontario.

Have you ever asked yourself: "Now that I'm bilingual, where do I go from here?"
 Ask no longer. The next rung up the ladder of linguistic delights is now labelled *duodemilingualism*! And you can be standing on it as soon as you pick up a smattering of Swahili, Malayalam, Afrikaans, Swedish, Spanish, Hungarian, Portuguese, Cantonese, or whatever third tongue you have always yearned to learn.
 As you may have noticed above, Ray Nakamura has given the boot to the *bi* in *bilingual* in favour of *duo*, which now marches arm-in-arm down Alliteration Alley with the other prefix, *demi*.
 But if we chop off *duo*, Nakamura's neologism suddenly shrinks to *demilingual* (knowing part of one language), giving us yet another possible candidate for entry into the English language. Demilingualism would be most prevalent among infants who are just learning how to talk: "Little Johnny knows over a dozen words now! He's already demilingual!"
 To compensate for a limited vocabulary, demilingual infants also grunt, groan, gurgle, chortle, howl, shriek, purr, coo, chirp, and whine.
 Of course, if a child is learning two mother tongues at the same time (or one mother tongue and one father tongue), the word we need is *demihemilingual* (from Greek: *hemi*—half).
 And if (Heaven forbid) the child is learning *three* mother tongues all at once, he or she could be said to be *demihemisemilingual* (from Latin: *semi*—half).
 Either that, or hopelessly confused!
 But if this child grows up to be a musician, he or she will feel right at home. According to the *Harvard Concise Dictionary of Music,* an eighth note is a quaver, a sixteenth note a semiquaver, a thirty-second note a demisemiquaver, and a sixty-fourth note a hemidemisemi-

44 duodemilingual

quaver. That last one is known in French as a *quadruplecroche*. And I thought only spiders had four crotches.

elephantephone

(ĕl-ĕ-FĂN-tĕ-fōn) noun.
A person who can imitate the trumpeting and bellowing of an elephant.
(Greek: *elephas*—elephant; *phone*—sound)
Coined by the author.

Soon after the passage of the Official Languages Act by the Canadian federal government in 1969, the terms *anglophone* (someone who speaks English) and *francophone* (someone who speaks French) achieved fame from coast to coast. Elsewhere in this dictionary you can find *swinephone* (for someone who speaks Pig Latin or, possibly, someone who hogs the telephone). But to find an *elephantephone*, you should go to Africa. That's where you'll find the greatest elephantephone of them all: TARZAN!!! With a single elephantephonic blast from his mighty vocal chords, an entire herd of elephants would come thundering and crashing through the jungle to rescue Jane and him from the clutches of almost certain death.

And for as long as old movies keep running on television, Tarzan will continue to bellow across the screen. But back in his younger days, as we discover in the "You Asked Us" column of *The Canadian* (Feb. 11, 1978), he needed some help in getting it out:

> For the famous yell we know today, Metro-Goldwyn-Mayer's sound department used the howl of a hyena, the bleat of a camel, the growl of a dog and the pluck of a violin's G-string. Each sound was played a fraction of a second after the previous one, all of them over Johnny Weissmuller's yodel, which was played an octave higher and somewhat slower. Both Weissmuller and later Tarzan Lex Barker learned to imitate the eerie sound so well themselves that the mechanical additives were not required. Hope they didn't disturb the neighbors.

But there's one time of the year when even Tarzan doesn't have much control over the elephants—and that's when the marula fruit ripens. These tasty tidbits are found in trees in Africa, and elephants find them irresistible. They'll even stand on their hind legs to reach the fruit, and after gorging themselves, they head for the nearest river to drink gallons of water.

elephantephone

The juice from the fruit then begins to ferment as the stomach turns into a giant still. When the alcohol reaches the bloodstream, the elephants turn into staggering, bellowing drunks. On one of these binges, an elephant in an African game preserve sat on and flattened a Volkswagen (the two Germans inside got out in the nick of time). When the intoxication begins to wear off, the elephants find some tall grasses where they can go to sleep—presumably to awaken the next morning with an elephantine hangover.

If all this makes you hungry as well as thirsty, you might consider the following recipe by Jack Rickel which appeared in the *Mark Twain Library Cookbook,* Volume Two:

Elephant Stew

1 elephant (medium size)
2 rabbits (optional)
salt and pepper to taste
brown gravy (lots)

Cut elephant into small bite-size pieces. This will take about two months. Reserve the trunk; you will need something to store the pieces in. Add enough brown gravy to cover. Cook over kerosene fire for about 4 weeks at 465 degrees. This will serve about 3,800 people. If more are expected, the two rabbits may be added. But do this only if necessary, as most people do not like to find [hare] in their stew.

et

(ĕt) pronoun.
A sexually non-declarative third person singular pronoun. *Et* is the nominative and objective case form, *ets* is the possessive, and *etself* is the intensive and reflexive. The plural is *they, their, theirs, them,* or *themselves.*
(*et* is derived from the *e* in *he* and *she* and the *t* in *it*)
Coined by Aline Hoffman, Sarnia, Ontario.

In an article written for ManuLife's in-house *News Letter*, Carol Gold tells us why *et* was born:

> Suppose you're writing a nursing manual—it's natural, since the majority of nurses are female, to use the feminine pronoun. But that leaves out the good number of male nurses who'll be reading it. If you're writing to insurance agents, it's most natural to use the male pronoun, since most agents are men. But since the Company is actively recruiting women as agents, are you going to make them feel left out?
> The problem seems insoluble.
> But wait! What word through yonder dictionary breaks? It's a noun! It's a verb! No! It's a sexually non-declarative pronoun!

It's also the shortest entry in *Brave New Words: et.* Aline Hoffman coined it when she was writing a novel for her Master's Degree in Writing at John Hopkins University. She simply took the *e* from *he* and *she* and the *t* from *it*. *Voilà*! *Et* was born.

To show us why the English language is in desperate need of this new pronoun, Aline asks us to consider the following "etless" sentences:

> Husband to wife: "I met a friend downtown today and we stopped for a drink. And they told me the most incredible story!"
> *The mistake is the use of the plural pronoun "they" to avoid declaring the sex of the friend—for whatever reason.*
> "A nurse is the one who has the most direct everyday contact with hospital patients. She makes their beds, administers their

> medication and simply *listens* to them."
>
> *The mistake is the use of the exclusive feminine pronoun "she." There are a large number of male nurses.*
>
> "The credibility of the image of the sculptor in his garret, nourished solely by inspiration from above, will be with us for awhile yet. But it's good to know that he's slowly being liberated."
>
> *At this time, the President of the Sculpture Society of Canada is a woman. The mistake is the use of the exclusive male pronoun "he."*
>
> "One must realize that if he or she is going to be great, he or she must be ready to sacrifice several needs, basic needs."
>
> *This sentence avoids the use of an exclusive pronoun but at the cost of fluidity.*

Aline hastens to point out that "some dictionaries define 'it' as a pronoun referring to a person, but there is little evidence that this word is used commonly in this way. In fact, referring to someone as an 'it' is more commonly considered an insult. Therefore, there is no word, at present, to fill the gap cited in the examples [above]."

Now let's read these sentences once again to see *et* in action:

> Husband to wife: "I met a friend downtown today and we stopped for a drink. And et told me the most incredible story!"
>
> "A nurse is the one who has the most direct everyday contact with hospital patients. Et makes their beds, administers their medication and simply *listens* to them."
>
> "The credibility of the image of the sculptor in ets garret, nourished solely by inspiration from above, will be with us for awhile yet. But it's good to know that et's slowly being liberated."
>
> "One must realize that if et is going to be great, et must be ready to sacrifice several needs, basic needs."

With these examples, Aline rests her case (oops! . . . *ets* case).

Grappling with the same problem Aline tackled, Jocelyn Classey of Toronto writes:

Dear Mr. Sherk:

Surely a pressing need is for a pronoun meaning *he or she* and here I have failed. I've tried *hesh* but people think you mean "Shut up!"; *heesh* is just about as awkward as the original, and *they* won't do because it's plural. Your students might enjoy the problem presented by:

"Everyone in the room was blowing his nose." (no females present?)

". . . his or her nose." (ugh!)

". . . their nose." (a nose belonging to more than one person?)

". . . their noses." (more than one nose per person?)

explunge

(ĕx-PLŬNJ) verb.
To use a plunger to clear a clogged toilet. "Don't use the bathroom! The toilet has to be explunged first!"
(Latin: *ex*—out of + *plunger* from Latin: *plumbum*—lead)
Coined by the author.

The next time your toilet backs up on you, grab a plunger and start explunging. Whatever's blocking it has to be gotten out of there and it's the *out of* which gives us the Latin prefix *ex* in front of *plunge*.

You may have spotted the similarity between *explunge* and *expunge,* a verb which, according to *The Webster Universal Dictionary,* means "to erase, wipe out, obliterate, or cancel." The only difference in spelling between *explunge* and *expunge* is the letter *l*, which has the same shape as the downpipe under your plugged-up toilet.

Back in the Middle Ages, no one did any explunging because toilets at that time had no drain pipes. As often as not, you simply answered the call of nature into a bucket of water, then tossed the whole sloppy mess out through the nearest window. If that window was on the second floor overlooking a street, you were expected to shout "Gardez l'eau!" (Watch the water!)

Because many second storey windows jutted out over the first, it became common practice for a lady to walk by under the protective overhang while her gentleman friend braved the elements out in the open. A shower of effluvia was a small price to pay for a young man anxious to display his gallantry.

Plumbiphiles (or is it *plumbiphiliacs?*) will enjoy wading through the pages of Wallace Reyburn's *Flushed with Pride*, the definitive biography of Thomas Crapper, a sanitation engineer in Victorian England who (according to Reyburn) invented the modern flush toilet. In a review of Reyburn's book in *Newsweek* (December 1, 1969) we learn that Crapper was a force to be reckoned with in the speedy disposal of the unmentionable: "Crapper's Valveless Water-Waste Preventer passed its most critical public test in a demonstration at the Health Exhibition of 1884, achieving a superflush that completely cleared away ten large apples, a flat sponge, three wads of paper and four paper sheets stuck to the bowl with grease."

explunge

Thomas Crapper should have been called John Crapper because a washroom is often called "the john." That's not surprising when you consider John is the most popular given name in the Christian world.

But have you noticed that only one king of England has been named John? That's probably because King John (1199-1216) was pressured by his barons into signing the Magna Carta, which put in writing certain limitations on his royal power. Whether or not he really was a bad king, thousands of tourists flock every year to the field at Runnymede to see the very spot where he signed this historic document.

Not so very long ago, a man and his wife who were taking a whirlwind tour of Europe (three countries a day for nine days) arrived at Runnymede just in time to catch the tail-end of the tour guide's spiel: ". . . and here, ladies and gentlemen, is the very spot where King John signed the Magna Carta."

"When did he sign it?" asked the man's wife.

"1215, Ma'am," said the guide.

Then she looked at her watch, turned to her husband and cried, "Oh, no! We missed it by 20 minutes!"

foof

(fōof) noun.
Acronym for *Fine Old Ontario Family*. Also comes in handy in Ohio, Oklahoma, Oregon, and on the Hawaiian island of Oahu. Members of such families are known as *foofians*.
(for details of birth, see below)
Coined by Nancy Cummins, Toronto, Ontario.

Foof was born at a Toronto garage sale where Nancy Cummins and her husband Rodger purchased a magnificent old wooden mantelpiece that must at one time have graced the drawing room of one of Toronto's oldest and most aristocratic homes. Nancy wanted a fresh new word to describe her new acquisition (it was almost too foofish for words)—so poof! As if by magic, she came up with *foof*.

If you don't have the good fortune to live in a city, state, province, or country that begins with *O*, don't despair. Just change *foof* around till it fits. A fine old Louisiana family would be a *folf*, a fine old New York family a *fonyf*, a fine old Boston family a *fobfam*, and a fine old Montreal family a *fomfam*. But anyone falsely claiming to belong to such a family is a *flim-flammian*.

Foof, by the way, is the only palindrome in *Brave New Words*. A palindrome is a word or sentence spelled the same backwards or forwards. For the low-down on palindromes, see the commentary under *politdrome*.

footle

(FŎOT-l) noun.
A door handle operated by the foot. *Handle* and *footle* are antonyms which both produce the same result. Therefore, they are also synonyms!
(Old English: *fot*—foot + *le*)
Coined by the author.

If you've ever tried to open your car door with both arms full of groceries, you'll appreciate the need for *footles*. A footle can be built into the fender behind each door of your car. Then when you debouch from the supermarket, you simply stand on one leg, shove your other foot into the footle, give a little twist, and *voilà!* Your car door springs open.

But how do you stop other people from footling their way into your car? That's no problem. Just have a key built onto the tip of one of your shoes to unlock the footle (and be sure to wear the right shoes to the supermarket).

Footles already exist (although not by that name) as metal covers across the lower parts of doors in schools, office buildings, etc., to protect the doors from scuffs and scratches incurred by people who open the doors with their feet instead of with their hands.

And a different kind of footle can be found as a verb and noun in *Webster's Dictionary:*

> *Footle* (fōo-tl) *v.t. (Colloq.)* to bungle; to be incompetent;—*n.* twaddle.—footling *a.* (etym. unknown).

But my favourite *footle* is a verb that belongs on T-shirts for lovers who like to play footsie: FOOTLE WITH CARE.

forelog

(FŌR-lŏg) noun.
Work completed *before* it is required; the opposite of a backlog.
(Old English: *fore*—before; Middle English: *logge*—a log)
Coined by the author.

The Heritage International Dictionary gives two definitions for *backlog*: 1) an accumulation, especially of unfinished work or unfilled orders; 2) a reserve supply or source. In a frantic attempt to elbow its way into the English language, *forelog* is prepared to rip that second definition from the pages of *Heritage* and claim it as its own. If it succeeds, newspaper columnists can use this new word just before going on vacation: "Here's my forelog of articles, Boss. There's enough here to keep my column going till I get back."

fornicatorium

(fōr-nĭ-kă-TŌR-ē-ŭm) noun.
A hotel or motel with hourly rates for fornicators. Plural—fornicatoria.
(Latin: *fornix*—arch; *orium*—place where)
Coined by Paul Dodington, Port Carling, Ontario.

In her book *More About Words,* Margaret Ernst sheds new light on an old practice:

> In ancient Rome, brothels were in a cave or under an arch, so the word *fornix* came to mean a brothel, and gave us the derivation of *fornicate.*
>
> Technically there is a difference between *fornication* and *adultery, fornication* being defined as voluntary sexual intercourse between *unmarried* men and women; in *adultery,* at least one party is married. But I am reminded of the old story about the New England farmer who was asked about this distinction by his son. He answered: "Well, I've tried 'em both, and there ain't no difference."

One of the most notorious fornicators in ancient Rome was Julia, daughter of the Emperor Augustus. In *The Natural History of Love,* Morton M. Hunt supplies a few spicy details:

> Julia developed an irresistible desire for pleasure and folly. Her first husband having died when she was little more than a child, Augustus married her off, when she was eighteen, to Marcus Vipsanius Agrippa, his faithful deputy, general, and builder of aqueducts, who was by that time wealthy, middle-aged, and tolerant. Julia, in hot-blooded revolt against spinning and weaving, took advantage of this to become the leader of the fast young set, and made her home a center of gay parties and luxurious display.
>
> Julia increasingly surrendered herself to a life of unbridled orgiastic debauchery. Rumours of her sexual escapades even reached the ears of her father, the Emperor himself. For years he refused to believe these wild tales: "As to the stories of adultery, Augustus was

fornicatorium 56

reassured by the fact that she dutifully brought forth no less than five children, all resembling her husband. According to rumor, Julia herself had a frank explanation of this flawless record: 'I take on passengers,' she is supposed to have said, 'only when the boat is full.'"

Special note for word lovers: According to Joseph T. Shipley in his book, *In Praise of English,* "there is no connection between *fornication* and *formication* (the tickly feeling of ants crawling on the skin) save that the god Zeus, the lusty protean lover, changed himself into a swarm of ants to seduce the nymph Clytoris."

foulese

(fowl-ĒZ) noun.
Foul language, either spoken or written.
(Old English: *ful*—filthy + *ese*)
Coined by Paul Dodington, Port Carling, Ontario.

Foulese is clearly a word whose time has come. When Rhett Butler told Scarlett O'Hara in *Gone with the Wind* that he frankly didn't "give a damn," his words almost ended up on the cutting-room floor. But that was in 1939. Over the past 40 years we have been wading through (some would say drowning in) a rising tide of foulese—a veritable cornucopia of pornography (or, as *Time* magazine once put it, a *pornucopia*). Foul and filthy words and phrases have been flung daily at our numbed and saturated senses. Even the ultimate four-letter Anglo-Saxon expletive is rapidly losing its punch through overuse.

O f__, where is thy sting?

But let's face it. The so-called F-word is still a shocker in many polite circles. Yet such was not always the case. On this very point, while writing an article on foul language among children for the Feb./Mar. 1979 issue of *Quest* magazine, Teddi Brown consulted University of Toronto Linguistics Professor Jack Chambers:

> He [Professor Chambers] picked up his chalk and went to the blackboard and wrote *fykan*. "That's where it comes from," he said, "the old Anglo-Saxon word meaning 'to plant seed.'" He explained that by the year 1200 A.D., *fykan* had switched to its present spelling and meaning, but it was still a good, sensible word and nothing to be snickered at. A religious play of the time included a perfectly ordinary character called John Le F__er. Then the Victorians got hold of the F-word and made it dirty. So who knows? A hundred years from now John Le F__ er may be back in good standing.

Meanwhile, euphemisms such as *shucks, phooey, dam,* and *heck* are still popular, especially with people in public life. On February 16, 1971, Canadian Prime Minister Pierre Trudeau was accused of having used an obscene four-letter word on the floor of the House of

foulese

Commons in Ottawa. Trudeau denied the charge by saying he had merely mouthed—but not uttered—the words "Fuddle-duddle." A member of the Opposition quickly quipped, "The prime minister wishes to be obscene and not heard."

Readers hoping to find filthy samples of foulese between the covers of *Brave New Words* will be disappointed. This dictionary is as clean as the King James Version of the Bible—and certainly cleaner than Shakespeare. This same standard of linguistic cleanliness was scrupulously observed by Dr. Samuel Johnson in his famous *Dictionary* (published in 1755):

> Johnson did not include [vulgar words] in his dictionary. They say that a pair of very proper ladies approached him at a literary tea and declared: "We see, Dr. Johnson, that you do not have those naughty words in your dictionary." To which he replied: "And I see, dear ladies, that you have been looking for them." [William and Mary Morris, *Harper Dictionary of Contemporary Usage*.]

But sometimes we can stumble into foulese by accident. Graham Walker, a Toronto teacher many years my senior, once gave me some wise advice on the teaching of the third person singular pronouns: "Bill," he said, "never forget to include the word 'and' when teaching 'He, she, and it.' If you leave it out, you'll bring the roof down because your students will hear 'He shee-it!' "

fuzztache

(FŬZZ-stăsh) noun.
A moustache on a young man before he starts to shave.
(contraction of *peach fuzz* and *moustache*)
Coined by Mario Bartoletti, Sunderland, Ontario.

Whatever you're interested in, there's a moustache to suit you—whether you grow it on or glue it on.

60 fuzztache

One day in downtown Toronto, *Toronto Star* columnist Gary Lautens noticed a man walking down Yonge Street with only half a moustache (a *semistache*). The next day in his column, Lautens offered several possible explanations for this bizarre behaviour:

- While making an end table in his home workshop, the gentleman in question had leaned too close to the electric saw. . . .
- He is working up an act for a circus side show in which he is to be advertised as Charlie-Margaret, "half-man, half-woman."
- While shaving after a wild night on the town in which he tossed back 38 double zombies and two quarts of Baby Beaver wine, his shaky hand slipped and he Schicked half his moustache. . . .
- A nasty variety of white grub has infested what was once a full-sized moustache and eaten its way half through the former pride and joy.

And if our half-hairy fellow was having a wild fling with "Hot Lips" Hoolihan from the M.A.S.H. show, Lautens is ready with the perfect explanation: "While saying goodnight to a loved one, the man became so passionate one of his kisses set his moustache on fire and half of it burned down before firemen brought the blaze under control."

galoosh

(gă-LOOSH) noun.
The sound of horses galloping across a shallow stream. "Sheriff! They galooshed that-a-way!"
(onomatopoetic)
Coined by the author.

Even if the horses are wearing rubber galoshes, it takes only a little water in a stream to change *clippity-clippity-clippity* into *galoosh-galoosh-galoosh.* If the horses are not in a hurry, they might canter across the stream instead of galloping. If that's the case, the sound would be *canteroosh-canteroosh-canteroosh* (the extra syllable slows them down).

A gallop is faster than a canter but that's not the only difference between these two words. Gallop comes from the French *galoper* and is an example of onomatopoeia because it sounds like what it means. But canter is short for *Canterbury gallop,* the leisurely pace of pilgrims riding on horseback to Canterbury Cathedral.

These pilgrims probably carried with them a decanter of wine to slake their thirst on the way to Canterbury—but decanter does not mean climbing down off your horse to have a drink. It comes from the Latin *de* (from) and *canthus* (the rim of a cup).

But what special attraction did Canterbury hold for pilgrims? A visit to Canterbury Cathedral became *de rigueur* for the followers of Christ after the Archbishop Thomas à Becket was murdered there by four knights four days after Christmas in the year 1170. Immediately after his death a rash of miracles broke out all over England. According to Thomas B. Costain in *The Conquerors,* "miracles of all kinds were performed by his blood, which had been saved in some quantity. It was given away in single drops. A receptacle containing no more than a drop would suddenly be seen to have filled, and this fluid would possess the full potency of the original. For centuries thereafter there were in existence quantities of the Water of St. Thomas, as it was called, and the power to create miracles was still in it."

Within two years of his death, Becket was canonized by the Pope and thus became known as Saint Thomas. For hundreds of years afterwards, the three roads leading into Canterbury were jammed

galoosh

with pilgrims—men, women, and children—from all over England, and indeed from all over Europe. All wanted to worship at the tomb of the martyr. According to Costain, "it has been estimated that as many as one hundred thousand pilgrims walked to Canterbury in a single year."

Today, about two million people a year visit this holy site. But most of them are not called pilgrims—they're called tourists. They come by car, bus, train, or plane. Very few arrive on foot or on horseback.

But with our dwindling supplies of oil, the horse may stage a comeback (horses are even now beginning to regain a hoofhold in the logging camps of British Columbia). And so the day may not be far distant when pilgrims and tourists alike head for Canterbury with a clippity-clop. Pilgrims might take their time getting there but tourists are always in a hurry. They won't canter when they can gallop. And when you consider the amount of rain that falls in England, they won't just be galloping. They'll be *galooshing!*

gnurn

(nŭrn) noun.
A totally useless ornament, often seen in the interiors of ostentatious automobiles.
(born out of spontaneous verbal combustion)
Coined by Arnold Korne, Willowdale, Ontario. Korne, 44, has owned over 500 cars (but not all at once). Many gnurns have passed through his hands.

In keeping with the meaning of the word itself, the silent g in *gnurn* is strictly ornamental, as is the g in gnarl, gnash, gnat, gnaw, gneiss, gnome, gnosis, and gnu. To give credit to Arnold Korne for coining this new word, we can also spell it *knurn,* with the k standing for his last name. That k is just as silent as the k in knack, knapsack, knave, knead, knee, knell, knickerbockers, knick-knack, knife, knight, knit, knob, knock, knoll, knot, know, knowledge, and knuckle. A third possible spelling would be *pnurn* with the p from pneumatic, pneumatology, pneumatometer, pneumonectomy, and pneumonia.

Those g's and k's and p's were not always as quiet as they are today. According to Edna Furness in *Spelling for the Millions:*

> Many modern English words have silent letters, which were pronounced in Anglo-Saxon and Middle English times. For example, the k in knight, knit, and knot and the g in gnaw and gnarl were all pronounced centuries ago. Moreover the gh in right, sight, and tight were once pronounced. Through the centuries, these sounds disappeared, but the letters have remained. . . . Many words of Greek origin have silent first letters which were pronounced in Greek. Examples are psalm, phthisical, psychiatry, pneumonia, mnemonic, and ptomaine.

Not many words have three different spellings but *gnurn/knurn/pnurn* is one of them. Yet this is small potatoes compared to *pugree,* which *The Webster Universal Dictionary* defines as "a kind of scarf worn [in India] round a hat to keep off the sun." No fewer than five additional spellings are listed: pugaree, puggaree, puggree, puggery, and puggry.

Such overwhelming choice was once commonplace in the English

63

gnurn

language. As Edna Furness points out, "before the advent of printing, you might spell button any way you fancied, writing it *button, butowne,* or *botheum,* as you preferred, or inventing your own spelling if you liked it better. For dinner you might eat *mutton, moltoun, motone, mottone, motton, motoun, motene, mouton, motown, muttoun,* or *mutten.* At least the printer eventually established that it was button and mutton." But standardized spelling did not arrive overnight. The printing press had been in England over a hundred years before Shakespeare began writing his plays—yet they say he had 13 different ways of spelling his own name.

g'orch

(gork) internerb. Rhymes with *cork*.
A command to music students to assemble for an orchestra rehearsal.
(contraction of "Go, orchestra!")
Coined and used regularly by David Ford, Head of Music Department, North Toronto Collegiate Institute, Toronto, Ontario.

G'orch is today's best linguistic bargain because it gives you three parts of speech for the price of one. It is, to coin a word, an *internerb* (part *inter*jection, part *n*oun, and part *verb*). As a contraction of "Go, orchestra!," *g'orch* is both noun and verb. As a four-letter interjection, *g'orch* is of immense therapeutic value—especially if the orchestra students are slow-moving and the conductor needs a handy expletive to give vent to his spleen.

For best results, *g'orch* should be bellowed like the stentorian blast of a foghorn: G'OR-R-R-R-R-R-CH!!!

If George Bernard Shaw (1856-1950) were alive today, he'd spell *g'orch* the way it sounds: *gork*. Shaw was a firm believer in phonetic spelling and left a large legacy in his will to promote spelling reform. To demonstrate the wide gap in English between spelling and pronunciation, Shaw devised the following word:

> GHOTI

Try as you might, you almost certainly won't pronounce it the way Shaw intended: *fish*. The *gh* comes from the *f* sound in *enough,* the *o* from the short *i* in *women,* and the *ti* from the *sh* sound in *nation.*

Be sure to order some ghoti the next time you visit a seafood restaurant. And wash it down with a steaming hot cup of *kawphy.* That beverage is spelled so badly, every single letter is wrong—yet the pronunciation is still correct. Such is the nature of the Inglish langgwidge.

T. S. Watt said it best in a poem which appeared in *The Manchester Guardian:*

> I take it you already know
> of TOUGH and BOUGH and COUGH and DOUGH.

66 g'orch

> Others may stumble, but not you,
> On HICCOUGH, THOROUGH, LOUGH, and THROUGH.
> Well done! And now you wish, perhaps,
> To learn of less familiar traps.
>
> Beware of HEARD, a dreadful word
> That looks like BEARD and sounds like BIRD.
> And DEAD—it's said like BED, not BEAD.
> For goodness sake, don't call it DEED!
> Watch out for MEAT and GREAT and THREAT:
> They rhyme with SUITE and STRAIGHT and DEBT.
> A MOTH is not a MOTH in MOTHER,
> Nor BOTH in BROTHER, BROTH in BROTHER,
> And HERE is not a match for THERE,
> Nor DEAR and FEAR for PEAR and BEAR.
> And then there's DOSE and ROSE and LOSE—
> Just look them up—and GOOSE and CHOOSE,
> And CORK and WORK and CARD and WARD,
> And FONT and FRONT and WORD and SWORD,
> And DO and GO, then THWART and CART.
> Come, come, I've hardly made a start.
>
> A dreadful language? Man alive,
> I'd mastered it when I was five!

Dreadful or not, David Ford prefers to spell his neologism *g-o-r-c-h* (after all, where would this new word be without the *orch* in *orchestra*?). And when he shouts it, it works. The orchestra students come a-running.

But once he gets them started, how does he get them to stop? Carole Paterson of Mississauga, Ontario, offers the perfect solution: because Ford starts his rehearsals with "G'orch!" he should finish with "Fin'orch!"

gruntometry

(GRŬNT-ō-mĕ-trē) noun.
Measurement by grunts (see below).
(*grunt* + Greek: *metron*—measure)
Coined by the author.

The story behind *gruntometry* is particularly appealing to all those who are disgruntled over the high cost of alcoholic beverages. In Pamela Harrison's *First Original Authentic Unexpurgated Great Canadian Quiz Book* we find:

> *Question:* "Five cents a grunt" never became acceptable English usage, but pioneers (in Canada) used it as a measure. What did it measure?
> *Answer:* Whiskey. A grunt was as much as a man could down in one breath.

Gruntometrists, unite! And tell your politicians that what your country needs is a good five-cent grunt again. Today's grunts can easily cost five dollars.

By the way, you might be wondering why *gruntometry* and *gruntometrist* have the accent on the first syllable and not on the second, as in *geometry* or *optometrist*. The answer is simple: the early pioneers vied with each other to see who could swallow the most whiskey in a single breath. If they went in for big grunts, why shouldn't we?

handymania

(hăn-dē-MĀ-nē-ă) noun.
An exaggerated desire or excitement induced by unfinished basements and/or hardware store advertising.
(Old English: *hand*—hand; Greek: *mania*—madness)
Coined by Brian Moccia, Mississauga, Ontario.

The *handymaniacal* (han-de-ma-NI-a-kl) do-it-yourselfer prides himself on the skill with which he can wield a hammer and saw. But let's face it. Even with the best of us, the hammer sometimes hits the thumb on the nail instead of hitting the nail on the head. And when it does, an ear-burning outburst of profanity often follows in hot pursuit. This can be embarrassing if your six-year-old son or daughter is standing within earshot.

Suffer embarrassment no longer! *Brave New Words* comes dashing to your rescue with an overwhelmingly powerful *but super-clean* swear word that you can use in any kind of company: RIGGAFRUTCH (see the entry under *riggafrutch* for details).

hek

(hĕk) noun.
A group of 100.
(Greek: *hekaton*—one hundred)
Coined by the author following a suggestion from Earl Hotrum, Toronto, Ontario.

After reigning supreme for hundreds of years throughout the English-speaking world, a whole cluster of words such as *inches, feet, yards, miles, pounds, ounces, quarts,* and *gallons* are now being elbowed out of the dictionary by North America's conversion to the metric system. One of the inevitable victims of metric conversion is bound to be the word *gross* for 12 dozen (144). If we round that off to the nearest metric-looking number, we're down to 100, a quantity which reduces a gross to a mere shadow of its former self.

But what do we call a group of 100? Let's take our cue from John Rutherford, a Toronto teacher who donated the word *dek* (a group of 10) to *Brave New Words* to replace the non-metric *dozen. Dek* comes from the Greek root *deka* meaning ten. The Greek root *hekaton* means one hundred. And so, if a group of 10 is a dek, a group of 100 must be a *hek.*

Even now, at this very moment, hardware stores are stocking nuts, bolts, nails, and screws packaged in heks. And with 100 main entries, *Brave New Words* is one hek of a book! But we can't call the Hundred Years' War one hek of a war. Why not? Because it didn't last for a hundred years. It was fought between England and France for 116 years (1337–1453).

Once *hek* catches on, it's only a matter of time before we call a centipede a *hekipede.* Then we can change *centipede* to *scentipede* to describe someone whose feet stink.

But if *hek* joins the English language, what will happen to *heck* (as in "Oh, heck!")? Heck is, of course, a euphemism for "Hell!" just as *shucks, darn,* and *phooey* are polite substitutes for those foul, four-letter obscenities, ____, ____, and ____. To avoid confusion between *hek* and *heck,* we could change *heck* to *helk* (a cross between *heck* and *hell*). By shouting "Oh, helk!" you get the best of both words. You give *heck* more punch and you make *hell* more polite. And if you shout "Hell!" just as a lady is entering the room, you can clean up your speech immediately by simply adding the letter *k* on the end: "Hell-k!"

impactipediphobia

(ĭm-păk-tĭ-pĕd-ĭ-FŌ-bē-ă) noun.
The fear of someone or something bumping into your already injured foot.
(Latin: *in*—into; *pingere*—to strike; *pes, pedis*—foot; Greek: *phobia*—fear)
Coined by the author.

This word was coined on special request. A student of mine named Jennifer Skillen had to undergo surgery on her foot—and for several weeks after, she hobbled around school with crutches and a large cast. In crowded hallways between classes, she found her foot getting accidentally jostled and bumped.
"Oooh! That smarts!"
She quickly developed a fear of getting her foot bumped again. One day after class, she asked me to coin a word for this fear. The result: *impactipediphobia!*

With such syllabic weight (eight syllables), you'd think this new word would choke anyone trying to get it out. But surprisingly enough, it skips, nimble-footed, ever so lightly off the tip of the tongue. You have to say it aloud a few times to fully savour its rhythm and euphony.

At a ski chalet you can use this word to meet the girl or guy of your dreams. Any word with 17 letters has *got* to be a great conversation opener. It might even be worth your while to deliberately sprain your ankle—if there's someone you want to meet badly enough. Armed (or should we say *ankled?*) with your cast, you can then regale strangers and friends alike about the horrors of being caught in the grip of impactipediphobia.

inverlegablist

(ĭn-vĕr-LĔJ-ă-blĭst) noun.
A person who can read backwards or upside-down.
(Latin: *in*—into; *vertere*—to turn; *legere*—to read; *habilitas*—cleverness)
Coined by Dominic DiStasi, Weston, Ontario.

Dominic DiStasi teaches Graphic Arts at Northern Secondary School in Toronto, where his students call him "the greatest Italian printer since Bodoni." It's not surprising DiStasi was the one who coined *inverlegablist*. Printers quickly learn to read backwards—and even upside-down—because all the letters in the type they set for printing are reversed.

"Watch your p's and q's!" This expression began with printers who were training their apprentices. Without these words of warning, a novice printer might set up "Please, Queen, spare my life!" and have it come out as "Qlease, Pueen, sqare my life!" If you want to give an old saying a new twist, try "Watch your b's and d's!" If you don't watch them, you might have Casanova going "to deb with a bedutante" instead of "to bed with a debutante."

English spelling is notoriously unphonetic and the early printers are partly to blame. In her fascinating book, *Spelling for the Millions*, Edna Furness explains why:

> [The printers] weren't so scholarly as the scribes they replaced, and they had less respect for refinements of spelling and style. They often varied their spellings in order to fit words onto a line, and readers would find words spelled several ways on a single page.
>
> One of the more interesting irrationalities we inherit comes down to us from William Caxton, the most important early printer. Caxton, in his search for good craftsmen, hired Dutch printers, who had practised the art for some time. They didn't know English well, and, following analogies from their own language, they supplied such spellings as *ghost, gherkin, ghospel, ghossip, ghess,* and *ghest*. As time went on, some of these *gh* words kept the unnecessary *h,* as ghost did; others,

inverlegablist

such as gospel, dropped the *h;* and some were changed, by analogy with French, from *gh* to *gu*—for example, guest.

Those early printers were the proud possessors of *inverlegablistical* (ĭn-vĕr-lĕj-ă-BLĬST-ĭ-kl) skills—but how about you? You can test your inverlegability right now by turning this book upside-down or holding it in front of a mirror. If you find you can still read it, you're ready for the next step. Turn to *invertographer* where you'll meet people who can *write* upside-down.

invertographer

(ĭn-vĕr-TŎG-ră-fĕr) noun.
A person who can write backwards or upside-down.
(Latin: *in*—into; *vertere*—to turn; Greek: *graphein*—to write)
Coined by the author in his sleep.

Invertographer first broke into print in the April 1976 issue of *Forum* (a magazine published by the *Life Underwriters Association of Canada*):

> Bob Hamilton of Toronto sells life insurance. Bill Sherk of York University teaches Word Power. Together, Bob and Bill have come up with a brand new word that all insurance salesmen should take note of.
> Bob mentioned to Bill one day that his boss can write upside-down. This unusual ability impresses clients a great deal—especially when a desk is separating client from salesman and the salesman writes facts and figures upside-down so the client can see them right-side-up.
> Bill suddenly realized that no word existed to describe a person who can write upside-down. He went to bed that night thinking about this gaping hole in our language. When he awoke in the morning, he had the word—*invertographer!*
> If you want to sell more insurance, learn to write upside-down. Your clients will be amazed every time!

Invertography is truly a great asset in business because if you can write upside-down, you can *read* upside-down (*see inverlegablist*). And if you can read upside-down, you can walk into your boss's office and read all his memos.

Perhaps the greatest invertographer of all time was Leonardo da Vinci (1452-1519). He filled over one hundred notebooks with his scientific investigations, all written in Italian from right to left ("mirror-writing")—presumably to conceal his ideas from prying eyes.

You're reading these words from left to right. If you read Hebrew, your eyes travel from right to left. And for a time in ancient Greece, words were written from left to right on one line and right to left on the next. This style of writing (in which even the letters were reversed)

invertographer

was known as *boustrophedon* (bōōs-trō-FĒ-dŭn) from the Greek word for "turning like an ox in ploughing."

Eventually, left-to-right triumphed and *boustrophedon* was abandoned. But if you want to see someone write from right to left today, just watch a TV weather broadcast in which the weatherman writes on the back of a transparent map. And I've heard of one lady who sends all her Christmas cards written backwards "just for fun." Her friends have to read them in the mirror.

So don't knock it if you haven't tried it. Grab a pen and piece of paper and try writing your name backwards or upside-down *right now!* You might be the proud possessor of unparalleled invertographical skills.

And if you are, fame and fortune could be waiting for you just around the corner! If Hollywood decides to film a multi-million dollar cinematic extravaganza based on the life of Leonardo da Vinci, you could audition for the lead part. You'd be one jump ahead of all the others who can only write right-side-up.

And if you look even a little like Charlton Heston, the part is yours.

janusian

(jă-NOOZ-ē-ăn) noun.
A person keenly aware of everything that's happening. One office worker to another: "You can't put anything past the boss. She's a real janusian."
(based on *Janus*, the two-headed Roman god)
Coined by the author.

Not everyone is a *janusian*. According to a remark overheard at a businessmen's luncheon, there are three kinds of people in the world: those who make things happen, those who watch things happen, and those who have no idea what's happening.

Janusian is based on Janus, the Roman god of gates and doorways. Because he had two faces, he could look in opposite directions at once. You've heard of people with eyes in the back of their heads? Janus was the first.

But *janusian* is not the only linguistic offspring of Janus. The month of January also comes from this Roman god because January is the month when we look back over the old year and then, armed with a fistful of New Year's resolutions, we sally forth eagerly into the new. *Janitor* also comes from Janus because a janitor, in addition to cleaning things up, is also expected to keep an eye on things—or, more precisely, two eyes one way and two eyes another.

If Janus were alive today, he'd be driving around in a 1947 Studebaker. Why? Because Studebaker was completely redesigned that year in a radical departure from contemporary styling. Instead of a rounded hump at the back (similar to the Volkswagen Beetle, which was designed in the 1930s—runningboards and all) the new Studebaker had a back end the same shape as the front. People used to say, "Which way is it going?"

kangamungle

(KANG-gă-mŭng-gl) noun.
A magical creature used after sunset by camp counsellors to hold little campers spellbound with tales of great adventure.
(probably a cross between a *kangaroo* and a *??????*)
Coined by Garry Fisher, Toronto, Ontario, who says, "There's not enough magic left in the world. We need to bring some back."

The kangamungle is not the only animal in Fisher's imaginary menagerie. As a counsellor at Camp Pine Crest near Torrance, Ontario, Fisher has enlivened many an evening campfire with stories about the antics of a *cholf* (half chipmunk, half wolf), *folf* (half fish, half wolf), *rolf* (half racoon, half wolf), and *squolf* (half squirrel, half wolf).

But of all these creatures, the kangamungle remains the most exotic and the most elusive. So elusive, in fact, that no one has ever seen one. Fisher alone has come the closest. Relentlessly and unflaggingly he has tracked this creature for days and nights on end—across frozen Arctic tundra and broiling tropical deserts, over windswept mountain passes and chasm-spanning hollow logs, through vine-entwined rainforests and piranha-infested rivers—but all to no avail. The kangamungle has always managed to stay just out of sight. All we have are footprints.

klickage

(KLĬK-ăj) noun.
Distance, speed, or fuel consumption measured in kilometres.
Klickage is a proposed new metric substitute for *mileage*.
(for etymology, see below)
Coined by Ernest McCallum, Sawyerville, Quebec.

When Mary Virtue, a librarian at Ryerson Polytechnical Institute in Toronto, Canada, was asked for the metric word for mileage, she discovered that the English language contains no such word! In French it's *kilometrage* and in Italian it's *kilometraggio*. The obvious English equivalent would be *kilometrage* but Miss Virtue decided that that word contained too many syllables for a streamlined language like English.

Convinced that someone—somewhere—could come up with a better word, she launched her Ryerson Library Cross-Canada Metric Word Contest on February 1, 1978. Before the February 15 deadline, over 500 entries had poured in from coast to coast. Canadian comedienne Barbara Hamilton selected the winner: *klickage*.

Klick (or *klik*) has been used as American military slang in Indochina for *kilometre* (see *Time*, July 6, 1970). But with his coining of *klickage*, Ernest McCallum brings to *klick* the linguistic glory it so richly deserves:

> *Klick* would suit the expressions "klicks per hour" and "klickage" relating to speed and distance.
>
> Many offshoots are obvious. For example, a speeder could be said to be going not "lickity-split" but "klickity-klick" and we could describe the speed of a vehicle running in reverse as moving at so many "klacks per hour."
>
> Naturally, a courier operating between two points would be going "klickity-klack."

Railroads will undoubtedly snap up McCallum's new word to describe the fuel consumption of diesel locomotives. Engineers will soon be comparing their *klickity-klackage*.

Running a close second to McCallum's klickage in the Metric Word contest was this entry from Andover, New Brunswick:

klickage

Dear Fellow Logotechnicians:

After hearing of your Metric Contest a few moments ago on Don Harron's CBC *Morningside*, I immediately put my shoulder to the wheel, my nose to the grindstone and my ear to the ground while allowing the windmills of my mind to run wild. The result of the mental and physical gyrations? EUREKA! ZUT ALORS! I have found it!

My entry: KIERAGE—or to be grammatically correct: KI'ERAGE (derived from *kilometerage*). KIERAGE rhymes with *steerage* or *peerage* and rhymes with *mirage* in French.

I submit the word KIERAGE for three reasons: 1) KIERAGE, like MILEAGE, is a two-syllable word accented on the first; 2) KIERAGE is an abbreviated form of *kilometerage;* 3) KIERAGE is more easily said than MILEAGE. The old MILEAGE required the lips to move from a closed position to open to achieve the "M" sound. But KIERAGE is uttered with the lips open throughout, trips lightly off the tongue, and requires less energy to say. In a time of energy conservation, every little bit helps.

I rest my case. My entry for your metric word contest is KIERAGE.

Yours sincerely,
D. Alan Riches

Thanks to Don Harron's cross-Canada *Morningside* radio programme, Alan Riches and *kierage* have landed right in the middle of *Brave New Words*.

But Don Harron is better known to millions of televison viewers in North America as Charlie Farquharson, the hayseed KORN announcer on *Hee Haw*. Charlie's wit and wisdom from "the back forty" have now been immortalized in Charlie Farquharson's *K-O-R-N Allmynack,* an indispensable guide to such vital matters as "indoor wild life, curing and tanning of kids, horrorscopes fer peeple under the infloonce, and advice fer the future and the pasture."

Under "Everybuddy will be on the metrecal," Charlie's comments on the metric system are delivered in pure barnyardese: "Now on accounta the gas shortedge, speed limits is gonna be upped th'otherway. Instedda ploddin along at fifty mile an hour, you'll be terracin' thru at a hundred kill-yer-meters. Won't be any faster, you mind, but you'll be thinkin yer gettin' more miledge fer yer money."

klickage 79

    Charlie himself did not enter the Ryerson Library Metric Word Contest but Donna Braby of Islington, Ontario, certainly did. No other entry matched hers for sheer linguistic variety: "To replace *miles per gallon* (mpg), we will use *kilometers per litre* shortened to KPL's or *kipples*. (If kilometers per gallon or KPG's, then it's *kippage*. Alternatives: *Kipplage? Kapples? Kepples? Kopples? Kupples?*"

    To bring all word coiners swiftly back to earth again, Kay Salmon of Don Mills, Ontario, writes: "I strongly believe that you would be doing the Canadian people a big favour if you let the Metric Conversion for mileage be *mileage*. This would be one less mind-boggling term to deal with. Thank you."

See also: *litrage*

lectaquaphobia

(lĕk-tăk-wă-FŌ-bē-ă) noun.
The fear of waterbeds.
(Latin: *lectus*—bed; *aqua*—water; Greek: *phobia*—fear)
Coined by Sam Rosenbaum, Toronto, Ontario.

Waterbeds have come a long way since the ancient Persians slept on goatskins filled with water. If you buy a king-size waterbed today, you'll have two hundred gallons sloshing around underneath you.

But not everyone is ready to take the plunge. Some people are lectaquaphobes and they're afraid of waterbeds for a variety of reasons: 1) "What happens if it springs a leak?"; 2) "What's this I hear about the sheets slipping?"; 3) "What happens if I want to move?" Waterbed manufacturers, being aware of these fears, have sought to turn lectaquaphobes into lectaquaphiles. Patch kits are available if you spring a leak. And good quality waterbeds have plastic safety liners.

lectaquaphobia

As for slipping sheets, special form-fitting sheets are now being designed to fit snugly around the sides of the mattress.

If you want to move, draining the water with a hose takes several hours. Rent a pump and you can get the water out in one hour. In "Some People *Love* Waterbeds" (*The Canadian,* April 15, 1978), writer Claire Gerus answers the question everyone asks:

> How is sex in a waterbed? It's all a matter of synchronizing your movements with that of the bed. One veteran likens it to "choreographing a difficult ballet," while another admits that although waterbeds are excellent for sleeping, he moves to his regular bed for lovemaking. Everyone agrees that it takes some getting used to. But, points out Andre Kocsis (co-founder of Halcyon Waterbeds, Canada's largest manufacturer), "There's more to sex than a waterbed."

One can't argue with that.

Fear-filled variations: *lectafoldephobia* (lĕk-tă-fōl-dĕ-FŌ-bē-ă)—the fear of being trapped inside a fold-away bed; *lectaquaglugephobia* (lĕk-tăk-wă-GLŬG-ĕ-fō-bē-ă)—the fear of drowning (glug . . . glug . . . glug) in a waterbed; *lectaquaretchephobia* (lĕk-tăk-wă-RĔCH-ĕ-fō-bē-ă) —the fear of getting seasick while sleeping on a waterbed.

Lexiconia

(lĕx-ĭ-kō-nē-ă) noun.
An island in the North Atlantic where new words are manufactured.
(based-on *lexicon* from Greek: *lexis*—speech)
Coined by Julian Bowron, Toronto, Ontario.

People keep asking me: "Sherk, just where in the hell are you getting all these new words?"

I used to mumble something about Latin and Greek roots but people always looked a little disappointed with my reply. They expected something more exotic. So now I give it to them.

All the entries in *Brave New Words* were first coined in a word factory on Lexiconia, an island sitting right on the *Polequator* (the 45° latitude line—see entry) in the middle of the North Atlantic about four hundred miles north of the Azores.

Strictly speaking, Lexiconia is not an island. It's a *sesquinsula* (an island-and-a-half, from Latin: *sesqui*—one-and-a-half, and *insula*—island) because it forms two islands at high tide and one island at low tide.

It was first settled in the ninth century by two groups of colonizers who were fleeing from the fury of the Norsemen: the McSherks of Scotland and the O'Sherks of Ireland. At first they supported themselves by farming the slopes and tending their herds of sheep and goats.

No one knows how the Lexiconians got into the word business because all the records of that period were destroyed in the Great Fire of 1555. It broke out in the middle of the island and would have burned everything down to the water-line if the tide had not rolled in six hours later and put the fire out.

Years ago, the Lexiconian scribes copied out all their words laboriously by hand. Today the Lexiconia Word Factory ("Words coined while you wait") is fully equipped with modern high-speed presses that churn out a million words a minute. Every hundred pounds of new words (they haven't gone metric yet) are boxed and crated, lowered into the hold of the *HMS Lexiconia,* and shipped all over the English-speaking world.

Lexiconia 83

But none of these words are sold directly to the public. All of them are auctioned off once a year to dictionary publishers who scramble feverishly to out-scoop each other on every new word. Each word goes to the highest bidder—just like tobacco, cattle, or antique

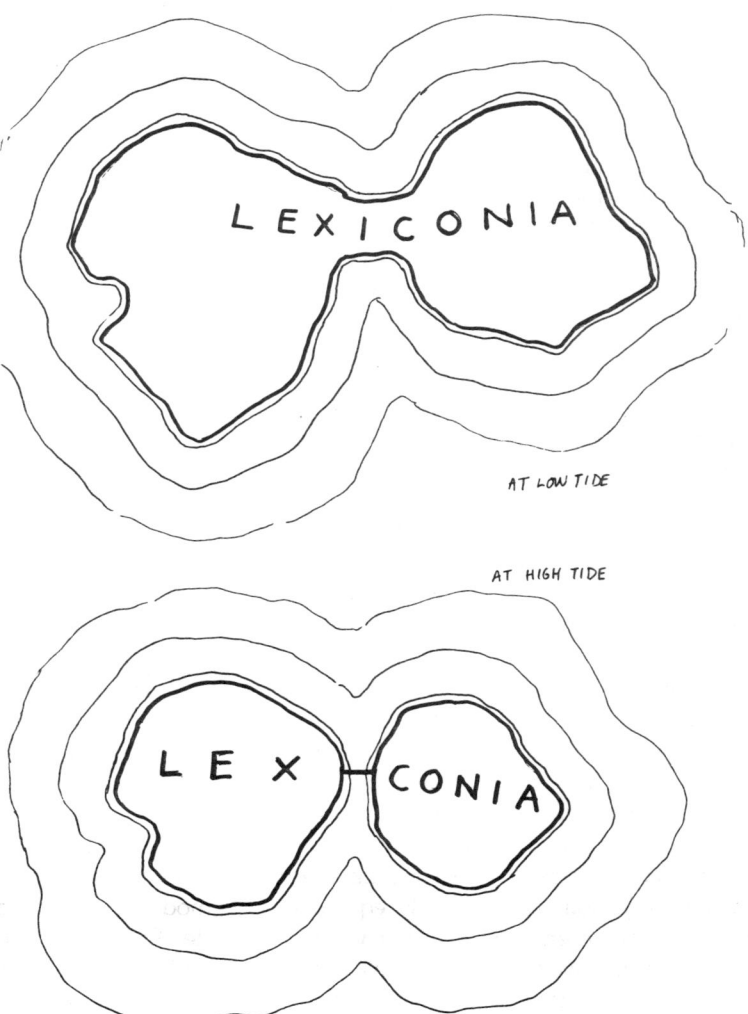

Lexiconia

furniture. Sometimes millions of dollars are riding on a single word. (Less than two weeks after it was coined, *Polequator* fetched more money than a Gutenberg Bible.)

But times are changing. To give the general public easier access to the new words thay crave, I have decided, as Word Lord of Lexiconia, to bypass the lexicographical wordmongers and release 100 newly minted words in *Brave New Words*. The Lexiconians won't make as much money under this scheme but it will certainly put Lexiconia on the map! Then they can recoup their losses by cashing in on the trans-Atlantic tourist trade.

If you're wondering why so few people know about Lexiconia, the answer is simple. It's because of the vegetation that grows there. It's ocean-coloured on top and sky-coloured on the side. So whether you approach the island by plane or ship, it's impossible to see it until you're almost there. In fact the first colonizers didn't see it at all until they smashed right into it.

But all this is changing. To help airline pilots find their way there, the name of the island has already been chiselled in granite on the top. Because the letter "I" would get submerged at high tide, it is filled with styrofoam and pivots on a vertical spiral shaft. Then when the tide rolls in, the letter I floats on the surface and slowly turns 90° to provide a footbridge for tourists walking between Lex and Conia.

It also comes in handy as a hyphen.

litrage

(LĒ-trăj) noun.
Fuel consumption measured in litres per 100 kilometres.
(French: *litre*—litre + *age*)
Coined by Robert A. Lane (P. Eng.), Toronto, Ontario.

"What word should we use for the metric equivalent of mileage?"
 That question was put to Mary Virtue, librarian at Ryerson Polytechnical Institute in Toronto, early in 1978. She soon discovered the English language contains no such word—although French has *kilometrage* and Italian has *kilometraggio*. To fill this gaping hole in our language, Ms. Virtue launched the Ryerson Library Cross-Canada Metric Word Contest on February 1, 1978 (see *klickage* for contest details). Because mileage has been used as a measurement of distance, speed, and fuel consumption, the search was now on for a metric word that would cover these three uses.
 As it turns out, metric fuel consumption requires a special word all its own. Robert A. Lane of Toronto explains why:

> The problem which has been raised by Mary Virtue, the Toronto librarian, namely, that of finding a replacement for the word "mileage" may have been answered already in the deliberations of Metric Commission Sector 4.03—Petroleum Refineries, Wholesalers and Gasoline Service Stations. The English language has in fact been relieved of a problem by these gentlemen because they have turned the whole concept upside-down. Starting in 1979, instead of measuring automobile fuel efficiency in terms of distance travelled on a given quantity of gasoline, we shall be using the volume of gasoline (i.e. number of litres) used to go 100 km. Thus L/100 km will replace mpg.
> I propose a simple solution—the simple word "litrage." My subcompact car gives me about 10—a nice decimal number.

Robert Lane's new word will start popping up in regular dictionaries faster than you can say "Funk and Wagnall." Distance and speed in the metric system, on the other hand, will be handled by *kilometrage*[*]

---

[*]Recently chosen by the Metric Commission as the metric replacement for mileage. This is an example of syllabic inflation: replacing a word of two syllables with one of four.

86 litrage

or *kilomage* or *kierage* or *kippage* or—my favourite and the winner of the Cross-Canada Metric Word Contest—*klickage*.

But does all this mean that *mile* and *mileage* are doomed to extinction? Not at all. Poets and songwriters will be using these words—especially mile—just as much as ever. A miss will still be as good as a mile. Santa Catalina will still be awaitin' for me, 26 miles across the sea. And Mammy will still hear those immortal words, "I'd walk a million miles for one of your smiles."

That word *smiles,* by the way, is the longest word in the English language because there's a mile between the first letter and the last. Metric lovers had better keep their hands off that one or they'll have us saying things like, "Every time he hears that story, he skilometres from ear to ear."

lupper

(LŬP-ĕr) noun.
A meal eaten in mid- to late afternoon in lieu of lunch and supper.
(*l*unch + *supper*)
Coined by Robert Marsh and David Wallace, Toronto, Ontario.

Lupper may need some help from *brunch* to get it off the ground and into our language. If you say you're going to eat your lupper, people will wonder what in hell you're talking about. For best results, try this: "Now that I'm on a diet, I'm down to only two meals a day—brunch and lupper."

Speaking of food, are you ever awakened in the middle of the night by rumbling noises in your stomach? And do you quell these rumblings with a belly-bulging visit to the refrigerator? If your answer is *yes,* then here's some news that may surprise you: because you're eating four meals every 24 hours instead of three, your body never undergoes any overnight fasting. Therefore, since you have no fast to break, you cannot, strictly speaking, refer to your first daylight meal as *breakfast.*

"But," you ask, "if I can't call it breakfast, what can I call it?"

No one knows. That word has not yet been invented. If you can think of one, fill out the word card at the back of this book and mail it in to the publisher. Who knows? Your word might pop up as a main entry in the next edition of *Brave New Words.*

masticambulistiphile

(măs-tĭ-kăm-byōō-LĬST-ĭ-fīl) noun.
A person who likes to walk and eat at the same time.
(Latin: *masticare*—to chew; *ambulare*—to walk; Greek: *philos*—loving)
Coined by Jeffrey Sherk, Toronto, Ontario.

Weighing in (and nearly breaking the scales) at twenty letters, *masticambulistiphile* is easily the longest entry in *Brave New Words*. But surprisingly enough, it is *not* the tongue-twisting mouthful it at first appears to be. After you say it half a dozen times, it rolls off the tongue as smoothly as a mouthful of well-oiled ball bearings.

Carnival time never fails to flush all your local masticambulistiphiles out into the open. You can see them strolling along the midway while gorging themselves on popcorn and candy floss.

Carnival, by the way, comes from the Latin root *carnis* (flesh) and provides us with such gems as *carnal* knowledge, *carnivorous, carnage,* and *carnation* (because it's flesh-coloured).

A close linguistic cousin of *carnis* is the Greek root *derma* (skin). That's why a skin doctor is called a dermatologist. You may have noticed that skin doctors never refer to themselves as *flesh doctors*—probably because the word *flesh* is heavily laden with lascivious, lecherous, libidinous, licentious, and salacious connotations. Fleshly pleasures are not for skin doctors—at least not during office hours.

One evening on *The Tonight Show,* Johnny Carson advised his television audience that the best branch of medicine to go into is dermatology. Your patients keep coming to you for years. They never fully recover and they never die off.

As Carson pointed out, "Whoever heard of anyone dying of terminal rash?"

mattresside

(MĂ-trĕ-sīd) noun.
The act of throwing out an old mattress. One spouse to another: "I'm ready to commit mattresside. I will *not* sleep in that lumpy bed another night!"
(*mattress* + Latin: *caedere*—to kill)
Coined by the author.

At last! A form of killing in which *no one gets killed!* What a welcome relief from all the violence and bloodshed you find smeared across the front page of your daily newspaper.

In addition to the fairly standard *homicide* and *suicide*, the English language is awash in such lethal specialties as *fratricide, sororicide, regicide, infanticide, genocide, patricide,* and *matricide*—not to mention *insecticide, pesticide,* and *verbicide*.

Fratricide (the killing of a brother) got off to a flying start just outside the Garden of Eden when Cain slew Abel—and the killing hasn't stopped from that day to this. Just look at all the fratricidal civil wars strewn across the pages of history. Sisters sometimes get killed too (even those in Holy Orders) and when they do, they are victims of *sororicide*.

But with the current trend toward unisex, *fratricide* and *sororicide* will soon be on the endangered species list. And what will replace them? What else but *siblingcide!* After all, murder is bad enough. Let's keep sex out of it.

Also on the endangered species list is *regicide* (the killing of a king or queen). With the ranks of royalty thinning out around the world, it's getting harder and harder for regicides to find a king or queen to assassinate.

But Charles I of England and Louis XVI of France knew how it felt to have regicidal subjects. Charles was dispatched with the swing of an axe while Louis—who wanted to be a locksmith instead of a king—suffered a mechanized demise under the blade of a guillotine.

Infanticide (the killing of an infant) was popular with the ancient Spartans, who were obsessed with rearing strong bodies to serve the state. Weak or deformed infants were left to die on the bleak slopes of Mount Taygetus.

mattresside

And *genocide* (the killing of an entire ethnic group) has been indelibly linked with Nazi Germany.

The most famous case of *patricide* (the killing of one's father) comes down to us from ancient Greek mythology and the famous trilogy written by Sophocles. Oedipus, son of Laius, King of Thebes, unknowingly killed his father and married his mother (making him perhaps the first *matrigamist* in history!). For a while, ignorance was bliss. But mother and son did *not* live happily ever after. A blind soothsayer named Tiresias finally spilled the beans, whereupon Jocasta (the mother) killed herself and Oedipus gouged out his eyes in remorse, then wandered through the world accompanied only by his faithful daughter, Antigone. Although Jocasta committed suicide, Oedipus in his own mind must have chalked up the death to *matricide* (the killing of one's mother) because he felt partly to blame for what had happened.

Although matricide (MĂ-trĭ-sīd) and mattresside (MĂ-trĕ-sīd) are almost perfect homonyms, the chances of getting them mixed up are just about nil. The context in which you use them should make your meaning clear.

And yet there is at least one case in recorded history when matricide and mattresside occurred almost simultaneously. The Roman Emperor Nero (54-68 A.D.) ruined a perfectly good mattress in his frantic attempt to get rid of his domineering mother, Agrippina. As John Trueman points out in *The Enduring Past*:

> He began by depriving her of her bodyguard and so harassing her with lawsuits that she left Rome. Three times he tried poison, and three times she escaped its effects. Then the floor above her bedchamber was made to collapse while she was asleep; yet still she survived. Finally an ingenious ship was built, a ship that would disintegrate and drown her. But Agrippina swam ashore. When news of her miraculous escape was brought to Nero he thought of the perfect solution. He pretended that the messenger had come to assassinate him and ordered his mother put to death.
>
> Even so, the records tell us, he was not rid of his ambitious mother. It is said that thereafter her ghost haunted him.

Incidentally, the word mattress comes our way from the Arabic *matrah*—a place where anything is thrown. Sound familiar?

meanderthal

(mē-ĂN-děr-thŏl) noun.
A wandering cave-man.
(*meander* + *Neanderthal*. See below)
Coiner unknown.

Meanderthal was phoned in to William French of the Toronto *Globe and Mail* on April 12, 1977, by an anonymous caller. Perhaps a meanderthal was passing through town. . . .

    You might think a meanderthal has no fixed address. Linguistically speaking, he has *two* addresses, one in Asia, the other in Europe. The

meanderthal

word *meander* comes from the Maiandros River which *winds* its way through western Turkey before debouching into the Aegean Sea. *Neanderthal* is the name of a valley in West Germany between Düsseldorf and Elberfeld. It was here that the skull of an early man was first found in 1856. The valley has thus given its name to Neanderthal man, a prehistoric European who died out about 20,000 years ago.

At least we *think* he died out. Maybe he wandered off with no forwarding address. . . .

mediability

(mē-dē-ă-BĬL-ĭ-tē) noun.
The ability of a book and/or its author to attract wide coverage in the media.
(Latin: *medius*—the middle; *habilitas*—cleverness)
Coined by Jack McClelland, President of McClelland and Stewart Limited, Publishers, Toronto, Ontario, who says that publishers no longer judge manuscripts, they judge "mediability."

Any book that gives a fresh new twist to something old and familiar stands a good chance of making a big splash in the media. The oldest profession in the world hit the bestseller's list with the publication of *The Happy Hooker* by Xaviera Hollander, a lady of the night who did all and now tells all. And one of the oldest books in the world has just been given a new facelift. *Olde Charlie Farquharson's Testament* is an out-behind-the-barn translation of the Bible written by Don Harron of CBC *Morningside*. Although it may not prove a match for The King James Version of the Bible (of which about 10 million copies a year are sold), Charlie's Testament is bound to attract the attention of the media. After all, how many other authors of the Bible have been interviewed on radio or television?

But sex and religion are not the only subjects with a high potential for mediability. The world of words scores high on this scale too—and *Brave New Words* is here to prove it. During the time this book was being compiled and written, it was the subject of a score or more of cross-Canada radio and television interviews and newspaper articles. And it's easy to see why: it's new, it's different, it's easily quoted, and it gives people a chance to get their names into a dictionary.

But how much mediability can a regular dictionary have? Plenty! *The American Heritage Dictionary of the English Language* was published in September 1969 and became the biggest-selling hardcover book of that year, outstripping even *Portnoy's Complaint* and *The Selling of the President*. In four months, 440,000 copies were sold. Aside from a promotional budget of *over one million dollars*, this new dictionary enjoyed some built-in mediability. According to *Time* (May, 11, 1970), "To comb out the neologisms and solecisms, the

93

94 mediability

editors consulted a usage panel of 104 unpaid judges, mainly journalists and other writers. Among them: Russell Baker, Vermont Royster, Red Smith and Dwight Macdonald. The wisdom of this move, apart from the publicity it brought the book, became apparent with the rave reviews that followed, some of them by panelists. . . ." And the editor himself was no stick-in-the-mud when it came to mediability: "The book's editor, William Morris, a onetime salesman who had a brief fling in summer stock, agreed to stay on after his contract expired and help with the promotion. He grew a silver Vandyke beard and plugged the book in a three-month whirlwind of appearances."

menuer

(měn-YOO-ĕr) noun.
A waiter, waitress, or *maître d'* who issues menus to restaurant patrons.
(French: *menu*—a list; *er*—one who does)
Coined by the author.

Because of its unfortunate phonetic resemblance to *manure*, the chances of *menuer* gaining acceptance in café society are slim in the extreme. One can imagine the following exchange if it did:

> Impatient customer (just arrived): "Where's the menuer?"
> Disgruntled customer (at nearby table): "On my plate!"

menuographer

(mĕn-yōō-ŏG-ră-fĕr) noun.
A person who writes mouth-watering restaurant menus.
(French: *menu*—a list; Greek: *graphein*—to write. The letter *o* in between the French and Greek roots represents the empty stomach you bring with you to the restaurant.)
Coined by the author.

Snugly ensconced in the heart of downtown Toronto is The Groaning Board, a restaurant ravishingly rich in its profusion of palate-pleasing pleasures. The gastronomic gourmet who owns and operates this haven of heavenly edibles is Harry Stinson, *menuographer par excellence!* Matching the food itself in taste, brilliance, variety, and razzle-dazzle is the Groaning Board menu, every word of which has flowed unstaunchably from the creative genius of Harry himself:

> No visit to the Groaning Board is complete without a romp on the salad bar: an eye-popping, mouthwatering, taste-awakening abundance of fruits, vegetables, grains, pastas, pickles, seasonings, concoctions, textures, flavours, and surprises. . . .
> HOT SALAD—with the guidance of the salad bar attendant, create a personal, edible Michelangelo, seasoned, cheese-strewn, and baked to a steaming crescendo. . . .
> MEXICAN MUSHROOMS—innocent bed of rice, overwhelmed by a throat-tickling torrent of mushrooms, beans, tomato, onions, and chillies (yes, ma'am, chillies; no foolin' around with this one) topped with a soothing oasis of sour cream, yoghurt, or cottage cheese. . . .
> PASTA—spaghetti à la Groaning Board—a generous noodly thicket, marbled with bean sprouts, slathered with a richly-herbed meat sauce, and dotted with olives and feta cheese. . . .
> JUMBLE PLATTER—God's gift to the indecisive—a palate-pleasing panorama of menu highlights; for the sampling couple or the enthusiastic trencherman. . . .
> YOGHURT PARFAIT—gobletful of ice cream, swimming in fruit yoghurt, marbled with chocolate syrup, deluged in cookie

crumbs, dripping with swirls of frozen yoghurt, dusted with coconut, and crowned with fruit. . . .

HAGAR SPECIAL—chunks of chocolate cake, merrily soggy with enthusiastic splashes of mead, baked with fresh fruit, surmounted by a crest of frozen yoghurt, and splattered with whipped cream, syrup and coconut. . . .

BAKLAVA—Middle-Eastern ground-nut pastry, wallowing in a decadent ooze of honey and syrup (how dare you?).

Newfanese

(no͞o-făn-ēz) noun.
An English dialect spoken in Newfoundland.
(contraction of *Newfoundland* + *ese*)
Coined by Mrs. John O'Mara, St. John's, Newfoundland.

When Australia first revealed its secrets to European eyes in the eighteenth century, a strange assortment of exotic plants and animals were found to be living on that ancient continent. Many of these forms of life had died out elsewhere millions of years ago. Australia turned out to be a giant living museum of natural history.

You won't find kangaroos or duck-billed platypuses on the loose in Newfoundland but you will find something almost as peculiar: *Newfanese*. Newfoundland may be Canada's youngest province (it joined Confederation on March 31, 1949) but it is also Britain's oldest colony. John Cabot claimed the New Found Isle in the name of King Henry VII of England in 1497, just five years after Columbus shouted the Italian equivalent of "Land ho!" A goodly number of words and phrases still in use in Newfoundland have been long dead in England—but were alive and thriving in the England of Shakespeare.

Newfanese is a mixture of modern English, archaic English, and invented English. For a sampling of Newfanese, we now open the pages of *Historic Newfoundland,* a booklet published by the Newfoundland Department of Tourism. Over 150 words (some of them rarely heard today) are listed, including:

ballycater—ice formed by spray on the shore
bannikin—a small tin cup
binicky—ill-tempered
bonnif—a young pig
crubeens—pickled pigs' feet
cuddy—a covered space in the bow of a boat
drook—a valley with steep wooded slopes
drung—a narrow, rocky lane
duckish—the time between sunset and dark
dwoi—a short snow shower
glutch—to swallow with difficulty

grumpus—the whale
gurry—blood and slime from fish
kingcorn—the Adam's apple of the throat
lolly—soft ice beginning to form in harbour
mauzy—misty
oonshick—a person of low intelligence
peeze—to leak in small bubbles
puddock—the stomach
scrawb—to tear with the nails
slinge—to stay away from school or work
squabby—soft as jelly
switchel—cold tea
twack—to examine goods and buy nothing
yaffle—an armful of dried fish
yuck—to vomit

But this list hardly scratches the surface of Newfanese. Scholars at Memorial University in St. John's are now preparing a "Dictionary of Newfoundland English" with 10,000 entries. In other words, it will have 100 times as many entries as *Brave New Words*. And since *Brave New Words* is one hek of a book (see *hek*), the "Dictionary of Newfoundland English" will be one hek of a hek of a book!

But Newfoundland is unique in more than words. The Newfoundland legislature follows a seating arrangement found nowhere else in the British Commonwealth. In every other legislature around the world which is modelled after the British House of Commons, the party in power sits to the right of the Speaker of the House while the members of the opposition sit to the left. In Newfoundland the arrangement is exactly the reverse. Why? Because for years, the fireplace that heated the room was on the left. The party in power thus sat on the warm side of the hall while the opposition members were, quite literally, left out in the cold.

niblings

(NĬB-lĭngz) noun.
Nephews and/or nieces who are each other's siblings. "I'm sorry we can't make it. We're visiting our niblings this weekend."
(nephews and/or nieces + siblings from Old English: sibb—kin)
Coined by Janet Collins, London, Ontario.

In defence of this new word, Janet writes, "I have always thought it easier to refer to my nieces and nephews who are siblings as *niblings*, a contraction which I find euphonious and convenient. It saves me from saying nieces and nephews all the time when I refer to one family."

Some people *have* niblings, some people *are* niblings, and some people are *niblingless*. Regardless of the category you fall into, be sure to heed the warning of the famous Chinese philosopher, Nib-Ling: "You mixed up but good if you count on fish *nibbling* on cheese and mouse *nibbling* on worm."

Norsex

(NŌR-sĕx) noun.
A missing Saxon kingdom in merrie olde England.
(contraction of *North Saxon*)
Coined by the author.

When barbarians overran the Roman Empire in the fifth century A.D. the 400-year-long Roman occupation of Britain came to an end. Soon afterwards, the Angles and Saxons of northwestern Europe began swarming across the North Sea looking for some cheap but attractive real estate. The Angles settled in the north of England and eventually gave their name to the entire country (*Angloland,* then *England*). The Saxons settled in the south and gradually divided themselves into the kingdoms of *Wessex* (West Saxons), *Sussex* (South Saxons), *Essex* (East Saxons), and *Middlesex* (Middle Saxons).

All of which brings us to *Norsex*. Surely *some* of those invading Saxons pushed further north to form a kingdom known as Norsex (Norfolk doesn't count because there's no *sex* in it). So far, unfortunately, not a trace of it has been found, not even in Northumbria.

Why no trace? There are three possibilities: 1) Norsex never existed; 2) archeologists have not been digging in the right place; 3) the climate of northern England twelve centuries ago was too cold for sex and the Norsexians wiped themselves out in a single generation.

Northumbria, incidentally, is the place where our present-day word *tawdry* originated. *The Heritage Dictionary* defines *tawdry* as "gaudy and cheap; vulgarly ornamental" and tells us the story behind this word: "From *tawdry lace,* short for *Seynt Audries lace,* cheap and gaudy lace neckties sold at fairs in honor of St. Audrey (died A.D. 679), queen of Northumbria, who died of a throat tumor regarded as punishment for her fondness for necklaces."

omnibibulous

(ŏm-nĭ-BĬB-yōō-lŭs) adjective.
Fond of drinking all beverages.
(Latin: *omnis*—all; *bibere*—to drink)
Coined by, but not descriptive of, Gerry Dunlevie, Toronto, Ontario.

> *Waiter:* "Would you like anything from the bar, Sir?"
> *Customer:* "Oh, just bring me anything at all. I'm omnibibulous."

As you can see, *omnibibulous* is the perfect word to have at your command at the end of a long, nerve-racking day. By the time you sink into a soft chair at your favourite restaurant, the last thing you want to face is another decision.

You can have the same freedom from choice when ordering your food—and here the English language has seen you coming and has a word already cooked up for you: *omnivorous* (from Latin: *vorax*—greedy to devour).

And so, when the waiter rushes to your table to take your order, just brush the menu aside and say, "I'm omnibibulous and omnivorous. Bring me anything you like."

But don't forget to mention how hungry you are. Otherwise you may end up with a nine-course meal when all you really want is toast and coffee.

omnibrow

(ŎM-nĭ-brow) noun.
A person whose cultural tastes range from high to low. For example, from fancy French restaurants to sleazy hot dog stands, or from Beethoven to punk rock.
(Latin: *omnis*—all; Old English: *brū*—brow)
Coined by Lister Sinclair (former executive vice-president of the Canadian Broadcasting Corporation), Ottawa, Ontario.

In the *Toronto Star,* July 8, 1972, Lister Sinclair talks about himself: "A lot of people have the wrong idea of me. I'm an omnibrow—not a highbrow, not a lowbrow—an omnibrow."
But in the 1950s a Toronto high school student named Bob Forbes (now a doctor in Chester, Nova Scotia) unwittingly came up with another definition for *omnibrow*. Forbes said that if he ever went bald, he would let his eyebrows grow long, then comb them straight back over his head, thus making the top of his head *all brow*.
He did concede there was one drawback to his *hair*-brained scheme: a very low forehead.

outro

(OUT-trō) noun.
An exit, departure, or fade-out. Radio announcer to studio technician: "On tomorrow's programme, we'll use this song for the intro and that song for the outro."
(*outro*—opposite of *intro*duction from Latin: *introducere*—to lead in) Coined by John Cargill, Toronto, Ontario, and used regularly by the students who broadcast the *Hot Air Show* three times a week at North Toronto Collegiate Institute.

A close (but not identical) synonym of *outro* is *egress* (from Latin: *ex*—out of; *gress*—step), a fancy word for exit. In *How to Build a Better Vocabulary,* Maxwell Nurnberg and Morris Rosenblum remind us that not everyone knows what egress means:

> Before his famous circus days, [P. T.] Barnum ran an equally famous museum in lower Manhattan. People liked the exhibits so much they just kept going around and around and staying so long that others couldn't get in. Being an astute businessman, Barnum tried to find a way out for himself and for customers who overstayed their welcome. Over the cage of the tigress and her cubs, he placed a large sign reading, "TIGRESS." Then, over a doorway next to the cage, he put up another large sign which read: "TO THE EGRESS." Thinking they were going to see some new curiosity, many of those in the crowded museum trooped through the door—and found themselves in the street!

P. T. Barnum was not the only one who could get people moving through an exit. Paul Dodington of Port Carling, Ontario, tells us of a friend in Toronto who suffers from claustrophobia whenever he rides in crowded elevators. One day he decided he just had to get everyone else off so he could have the elevator all to himself. Just before it reached the next floor (he was jammed into a corner at the back), he said in a quavering voice, "I think . . . I'm going . . . to vomit."

Then the doors opened. EVERYONE GOT OUT!—everyone, that is, except the would-be vomitor (the other passengers did not wish to become vomitees). Then the door closed and the now-happy claustrophobe was whisked away in privacy and comfort.

outro

Incidentally, the words he used to empty the elevator were often spoken in ancient Rome (in Latin, of course). Wealthy Romans who wined and dined all night long often made use of a vomitorium (yes, that's what they called it!), a room adjacent to the dining room where gluttonous epicures disgorged the contents of their stomachs so they could keep on eating hour after hour. One Roman even had a slave whose job it was to tickle his master's throat with a feather whenever his stomach was full.

oysterical

(oy-STEER-ĭ-kl) adjective.
Oyster-shaped.
(Greek: *ostreon*—oyster)
Coined by Alan Walker, Toronto, Ontario.

Oysterical is probably the oldest new word in this book. It was coined back in the 1960s by *Time* Canada journalist Alan Walker (now National News Editor of *Maclean's*) to describe the oyster-shaped council chamber of Toronto's new city hall, a building now famous throughout the world. Much to Walker's delight, *Time* printed his new word. "That was *Time* for you," Walker explains. "Nobody else would allow it."

oysterical

Toronto's new council chamber has more in common with oysters than shape alone. Both have hard shells on the outside and soft flesh on the inside. Both have indoor plumbing. And both can open their shells—the oyster when yawning and the council chamber when filled with irate citizens raising the roof. But unlike the politicians who fulminate inside the council chamber, oysters cannot produce an unlimited supply of hot air.

Once it gets into circulation, *oysterical* might broaden its meaning to include hysterical oysters. Then the author of a children's book could write: "When Ollie the Oyster saw the hungry starfish lumbering toward him, he became *oysterical!!!*"

And with good reason. Once a starfish wraps its five sucker-equipped legs around an oyster's shell and starts pulling, the oyster is doomed. It may take hours but eventually the shell opens. What happens next would make your skin crawl if you witnessed it. Instead of chomping and gulping the flesh of the hapless oyster, the starfish turns its stomach inside-out, thus passing it out through its mouth and toward the oyster's cold, watery flesh. Once contact is made, the digestive juices of the starfish go slowly to work until nothing is left but an empty shell. Then the stomach is retracted and the starfish glides away in search of his next meal. And thus ends the life of Ollie the Oyster.

But there are many more oysters where he came from. A female oyster can lay as many as 500 million eggs a year—and looking after a brood that big is enough to make any mother hysterical!

parsipetrolambulist

(păr-sĭ-pĕ-trō-LĂM-byoō-lĭst) noun.
A person who walks in order to save gasoline.
(based on *parsimonious* from Latin: *parcere*—to spare; *petroleum* from Latin: *petra*—rock + *oleum*—oil; Latin: *ambulare*—to walk)
Coined by Gwen Resnick, Toronto, Ontario.

With seven syllables and 19 letters, *parsipetrolambulist* is one of *Brave New Words'* polysyllabic heavyweights, exceeded in length only by the 20-letter *masticambulistiphile*. But these two words are small potatoes compared to a town in Wales called *Llanfairpwllgwyngyllgogerychwyrndrobwllllantysiliogogogoch* (sometimes called "Llanfairpwll" for short).

If we go straight to the heart of *parsipetrolambulist*, we find *petrol*, which comes from *petroleum* (Latin: *petra*—rock; *oleum*—oil), which in turn comes from the rocky bowels of the earth. But it's not just Mother Earth who has oil in her bowels. Whenever you're constipated, a well-oiled suppository will get *your* bowels moving again.

If you have ever wondered why *petroleum* rhymes with *linoleum*, you're about to find out. *Linoleum* literally means "oil cloth" (from Latin: *linum*—flax; *oleum*—oil). And of all the words in the English language, *linoleum* is one of the most pleasing to the ear. It rolls off the tongue like a mouthful of well-oiled ball bearings. In fact, a fellow once told me that if he ever had a daughter, he would name her Linoleum because the word is so euphonious. I hope he changes his mind because with a name like that, people would walk all over her.

Because of its enormous size (it stretches across nearly half a page), *parsipetrolambulist* takes up almost as much space as the big gas-guzzling dinosaurs now sitting lifeless in the driveway of every parsipetrolambulist worthy of the name.

But not everyone likes to walk in order to save gasoline. Those who don't have switched to smaller cars. And with steadily rising gasoline prices, the smaller the car, the better. The same holds true for words. Big, long, heavy words burn up too much energy; short, crisp words catch on faster and stick around longer. If *parsipetrolambulist* hopes to survive in an energy-hungry world, it will have to be downsized to *parsipet*: "Ever since that last price increase for gasoline, my husband

parsipetrolambulist 109

and I have been a couple of confirmed parsipets. And we're going broke paying for all the shoe leather!"

Many budget-conscious motorists became part-time parsipets following the Arab oil embargo of October 1973. But the shock and panic that followed that embargo prevented most people from noticing just how sexy the word *embargo* really is. Spell it backwards and you have the words of a girl with romance on her mind.

pekilar

(PĚK-ĭ-lăr) noun.
Any mispronounced word. "He'll never get voted into office. Every speech he gives is full of pekilars."
(for etymology, see below)
Coined by accident in 1849 in the Red River colony (on the site of present-day Winnipeg, Manitoba).

If you're looking for a Greek or Latin root in *pekilar*, you're wasting your time. This word was born in a little schoolhouse in the Canadian west over a hundred years ago. In his book, *The Selkirk Settlers in Real Life,* R. G. MacBeth tells us how it happened:

> . . . the success or failure of a teacher [in the Red River colony] was decided by the inspection and report of the trustees aforesaid. As these trustees were for the most part "plain, blunt men," whose . . . "dialect" was more or less affected by Gaelic, Salteaux, Cree and French influences, the lot of the teacher was not always a happy one. When Inkster was teaching in '49, the trustees came in to inspect, and one of them gave to the leading class in the school the word "pekilar" to spell. It had never been heard of up to that time, and so proved a "poser" for the whole class from head to foot, whereupon the trustee grew somewhat indignant and threatened to dismiss the teacher whose leading class could not spell "pekilar." The teacher, however, asked to see the word, and saved his official head by pointing out that it was pronounced "peculiar," which latter word was triumphantly spelled by the class, who thus vindicated the scholarly attainments of their teacher.

One hundred and thirty years later, I sat down at my typewriter in my home in Toronto to put the finishing touches on the manuscript for *Brave New Words.* I had written 99 chapters (not in alphabetical order) and had one more to go. I began flipping through my word files searching for that last, elusive word around which I would write my final chapter.

And then I saw *pekilar*. It had been lying buried in my files for over three years because it had no legitimate definition. Well, why not give

pekilar

it one? After all, when a word hangs in limbo for over a hundred years, waiting and hoping for someone to snap it up, the least we can do is to give that word a fighting chance. Words have been mispronounced every day since the English language began. We need a short and snappy little word to cover this problem. What better choice could there be than *pekilar*, which is itself an example of that which it defines!

Although the original *pekilar* was an adjective (as is *peculiar*), we have now changed it into a noun. The practice of using pekilars would be *pekilarity* (rhymes with hilarity) and a person so addicted would be a *pekilarian* (pĕk-ĭ-LAIR-ē-ăn). And a wife who nags her husband *pekilariously* would be a *henpeckilarian*.

Pekilarians often place the ĕm-FĂS-ĭs on the wrong sȳl-Ă-bŭl but comfort can be taken in the fact that some words give you a choice— even words of one syllable. One evening in my Word Power class I was explaining how the word *vase* can be pronounced either *vās* or *vawz*. Either way, the meaning is the same. "Oh, no, it isn't!" piped up a lady from the back row. "A *vās* costs under 10 dollars and a *vawz* costs over 10 dollars."

plouse

(plous) noun. Rhymes with *house*.
An unmarried person living on intimate terms with a member of the opposite sex.
(contraction of *playing house*)
Coined by Bryan Smith, Yarmouth, Nova Scotia.

Plouse will get some mighty stiff competition in the lexicographical sweepstakes from its synonym, *covivant*. Unfortunately, *plouse* rhymes with *louse** and may end up as a term of scorn and abuse, used only by persons who disapprove of plousical relationships: "I can't begin to tell you how disgusted I am. I've just learned that our daughter and her boy friend are a couple of plouses!" (The plural form could be *plice,* a highly unflattering term since it rhymes with *lice*.)

Canadian poet John Robert Colombo has suggested that *plouse* might improve its chances for linguistic survival if it switches from a noun to a verb. Instead of talking about a couple of plouses playing house, we could say they are *plousing*. And if they ever decide to end the relationship, they could be said to be *deploused*.

---

*Come to think of it, so does *spouse*. And if we add the letter *l*, we get *splouse* (a married louse?).

plumbiped

(PLŬM-bĭ-pĕd) noun.
A motorist with a lead foot.
(Latin: *plumbum*—lead; *pes, pedis*—foot)
Coined by the author.

If you think this noun is hot stuff at a traffic light, feast your eyes and ears on the clutch-popping, pedal-stomping, tire-squealing adjective, *plumbipedal* (plŭm-BĬP-ĕ-dl). With the accent on the second syllable (BIP!), those eleven letters are oozing with onomatopoeia! Say them aloud with the right emphasis and you can hear a plumbiped squealing away from a green light. . . .

114 plumbiped

Polequator

(PŌL-ĕ-kwā-tōr) noun.
The 45° latitude line, mid-way between the equator and the North or South Pole.
(contraction of *Pole* and *equator*)
Coined by the author.

Up until now, and with the sole exception of the Arctic Circle, the United States and Canada have been denied any special latitude or longitude lines within their boundaries. The equator, the Tropic of Cancer, the Tropic of Capricorn, the Greenwich Meridian, and the International Date Line are all located in other parts of the world.

But the Polequator passes through or touches 12 American states: Maine, New Hampshire, Vermont, New York, Michigan, Wisconsin, Minnesota, South Dakota, Montana, Wyoming, Idaho, and Oregon. It also touches four Canadian provinces: Nova Scotia, New Brunswick, Quebec (*le Pôléquateur*), and Ontario. It could become North America's newest tourist attraction. Over 50 million people can reach it by car in less than one day.

And on the far side of the Pacific, *over one billion people* could reach it in less than a week. Like a Roman highway it marches unswervingly across Hokkaido, Manchuria, Mongolia, the Soviet Union, the Caspian Sea, the Crimean Peninsula, Romania, Yugoslavia, Italy, and France.

Polequator

The Southern Hemisphere has a polequator too (45° South) but not many people live along it (those who do are known as *polequatarians*). It spans the chilly waters of the far southern seas except for a quick slice through Chile, Argentina, and the South Island of New Zealand. Australia, alas, is too far north. As a consequence, kiwi birds get the chance to hop back and forth across the line but kangaroos do not.

As a stimulant to the world's economy, *Polequator* could not have been coined at a better time. This new geographical term makes every map of the world obsolete. Just think of the riches to be reaped by publishers who come out ahead in the frantic stampede to issue the world's first polequatorized atlas.

And the size of the real estate boom staggers the imagination. As soon as Washington and Ottawa officially declare the 45° latitude line to be the Polequator, the price of land all along the line will skyrocket. Restaurants, hotels, motels, amusement parks, and souvenir stands will sprout faster than you can say *Polequatorization*. The insatiable demand for T-shirts and bumper stickers alone ("*We crossed the Polequator!*") will create several overnight fortunes.

If you want to cash in on what could be the last big land rush in history, start buying up property now while it's still cheap. . . .

politdrome

(PŎL-ĭt-drōm) noun.
A politician running for office.
(French: *politique,* from Greek: *polis*—a city; Greek: *dromos*—running)
Coined by David and Gary Ballentine, Toronto, Ontario.

As these very words are being written (April 1979), Canada is caught in the grip of a *politdromic* frenzy—a federal election campaign is now in full swing with hundreds of politicians running for office.

Meanwhile, south of the border, American politicians are running *in* office:

> These days, nearly half the Senate is running in office. The freshman Republican class are avid members of the shin-splint generation, and six of them suited up one morning at sunrise to puff on the mall. Despite a wind-chill factor of 0°, [the Senators] enjoyed their informal caucus. [*Time,* Feb. 19, 1979]

Why do they jog? According to Wyoming Senator Alan Simpson, 47: "It clears away the fog."

On the other hand, the Watergate scandal presented us with the spectacle of politicians being run *out* of office. And for someone who likes to run, that's almost as bad as running out of stamina.

As a new word, *politdrome* is getting off to a running start because it has several linguistic cousins who are members in good standing in the English language, including *aerodrome, dromedary, hippodrome, syndrome,* and *palindrome.* Through the Greek root *dromos,* all these words are related to *running.*

Aerodrome, for example, is a British term for airport, landing field, or airplane hangar. And where you find airplanes, you usually find runways. A *choo-choo-drome,* however, is something quite different. That's a person running along a station platform trying to catch a train.

If you're nervous about flying and don't like trains, maybe you should travel by camel. These "ships of the desert" come in two models: the one-hump *dromedary* and the two-hump *Bactrian.* The kind you want is the dromedary. For crossing the Sahara in a hurry,

117

the dromedary is unbeatable. Fill him with water and he can run a hundred miles a day.

Sharing the continent of Africa with the camel is the hippopotamus. At first glance you might think a *hippodrome* is a place where hippopotami run. Not so—although Alan Moorehead, author of *No Room in the Ark,* visited a place in Africa where hippos had to move extra fast: "On the Zambesi River I recall they had to run a launch up and down the water a few minutes before the plane came in to clear the hippopotami away."

Hippopotamus means "river horse" (from Greek: *hippos*—horse; *potamos*—river). And *hippodromes?* Originally they were race-tracks in ancient times where horses, often pulling chariots, thundered along at breakneck speed before crowds of cheering spectators: "Yea, Ben! Yea, Hur! Yea, yea, Ben-Hur!"

In modern times, *hippodrome* (according to Webster) has been "frequently applied to a racing-track of any kind; often, too, as the name of a variety theatre, cinema, etc." Before it was torn down in 1957, Shea's Hippodrome in Toronto hosted a long succession of silent and talking motion pictures. If any horses wanted inside, they had to buy a ticket just like anyone else.

Although it certainly sounds evil, *syndrome* has nothing to do with sin. It's based on the Greek prefix *sun* (together) and crops up in remarks such as: "Let's synchronize our watches" or "Be careful shifting gears on this oldtimer. It doesn't have synchro-mesh."

When we bolt *syn* onto *drome,* we have a number of symptoms that occur (or *run*) *together.* And with inflation steadily eating its way into our purchasing power, we now have the "shrinking candy bar syndrome." According to Olivia Ward in the Toronto *Sunday Star* (July 23, 1978):

> It's downsizing—the trimming of goods and services that cost the same as the old products but aren't as big, as heavy or as plentiful.
>
> Known as the "shrinking candy bar syndrome," downsizing is hidden inflation. . . . Hardly anyone is immune to the new Small Thinking. Cars shrink while prices go up, restaurants trim adult portions to kiddie size, magazines are less colorful, airlines have less elbow room—and yes, your chocolate bars really are shrinking.

politdrome 119

And now for a question that will send you *running* to the Old Testament: What were the very first words spoken in the Garden of Eden? You won't find them in the Book of Genesis but here they are, just the same: "Madam, I'm Adam."

That sentence can be spelled the same backwards and forwards (even the comma and apostrophe are reversible!). Such a sentence or word is known as a *palindrome* (from Greek: *palin*—back; *dromos*—running). Eve's reply was equally palindromic: "Oho!"

Some Old Testament scholars insist that Eve really said "Aha!" (another palindrome). And a Japanese linguist claims to have found proof that she said "Oso!" We'll probably never know for sure.

But one thing is certain. If Eve didn't like the looks of Adam, she should have said:

*A semi-palindrome (it sounds like one but isn't).

pwelgas

(PWĔL-gǎs) noun.
Acronym for the Seven Deadly Sins of *p*ride, *w*rath, *e*nvy, *l*ust, *g*luttony, *a*varice, and *s*loth.
Coined by the author.

Pwelgas is the perfect time-saver for a clergyman who preaches at more than one church on Sunday morning. If he finds himself running behind schedule at his first service, he can wrap things up all in one fell swoop by intoning, ". . . and lead us not into pwelgas . . ." as he dashes out the front door to a getaway car idling at the curb.

If our fleet-of-foot clergyman has a flair for the theatrical, he can make his exit far more dramatic. All he needs alongside his pulpit is a brass fireman's pole disappearing through a hole in the floor. When it's time to go, he says, "Lead us not into pwelgas-s-s-s . . ." as he slides down the pole, through the floor, into the church basement, and straight into the driver's seat of a waiting convertible (top down, please!). A spring-loaded garage door then swings open as he drives up a ramp and pours on the gas to get to his next church on time.

The *pwelgas-pole* (as good a name as any) provides a smashing finale for every hellfire-and-brimstone sermon. As their pastor plummets out of sight right before their dazzled eyes, the members of the congregation cannot fail to notice the symbolism—of how the gates of Hell open wide to devour all those who wallow in a decadent cesspool of *pwelgassery*.

The economy model: If parsimonious parishioners balk at the price of a pwelgas-pole and a Hades-red convertible, they can make do with a hole in the floor and a bicycle down below. Using the skirt of his clerical robe as a parachute, His Most Reverend can leap feet-first through the hole and float down onto the bicycle as gently as a feather falling into a bowl of soapsuds.

As soon as pwelgas becomes a churchhold and household word, it will quickly spawn a surfeit of suffixes including:

>*Pwelgassic*—Adjectival form of *pwelgas*.
>*Pwelgasite*—One who is guilty of committing all seven deadly sins.

Pwelgasiphile—One who enjoys committing all seven deadly sins.
Pwelgasiphobe—One who is afraid of committing all seven deadly sins.
Pwelgasorium—A den of iniquity.
Pwelgasoholic—A compulsive sinner.
Pwelgasify—(verb). To lead someone down the garden path past the point of no return. ("Help! I'm being pwelgasified!")

pyropecuniac

(pī-rō-pĕ-KOO-nē-ăk) noun.
A person who makes money from fires without starting them.
(*pyro* from Greek: *pur*—fire; Latin: *pecunia*—money)
Coined by the author.

The original *pyropecuniac* was a wheeler-dealer in ancient Rome named Marcus Licinius Crassus (112-53 B.C.). The city of Rome at that time had no municipal fire department, thus giving Crassus his big chance to show his flair for pyropecuniacy. He organized his own private fire department and rushed to the scene of burning buildings, then stood idly by and refused to put out the fire until the frantic owner agreed to sell him the property for next to nothing.

With his *pyropecuniacal* (pī-rō-pĕk-yoō-NĪ-ă-kl) wizardry Crassus soon made a fortune in Roman real estate. With his colossal riches he bought the votes of the Roman masses, allied himself with Julius Caesar, and climbed the greasy pole of Roman politics. His amazing career was suddenly snuffed out in Syria in 53 B.C. when he was killed fighting the Parthians.

Do we have any pyropecuniacs around today? Yes, indeed. Your local fire extinguisher and smoke sensor salespeople, for example. Every time a fire breaks out, they sell more merchandise.

But the members of your neighbourhood fire department do *not* qualify for this new word because they are on salary and get paid whether fires break out or not. Because they fight fires, we could call them *pyropugilists* (*pyro* + Latin: *pugnare*—to fight).

quadocular

(kwŏd-ŎK-yōō-lăr) adjective.
Wearing eyeglasses.
(Latin: *quattuor*—four; *oculis*—eye)
Coined by David and Gary Ballentine, Toronto, Ontario.

It's not easy to coin a new word beginning with the letter Q but David and Gary Ballentine (both of whom are quadocular) have done it. Gone forever is the faintly insulting "four eyes" to describe someone who wears glasses.

If you wear glasses and you clip sunglass lenses onto the front of them, you become *sexocular** (from Latin: *sexa*—six). And if you look through a pair of binoculars at the same time, you automatically become—you guessed it!—*octocular* (from Latin: *octo*—eight).

If you wear contact lenses, you'd be *contactocular* (kŏn-tăk-TŎK-yōō-lăr). And if you have a grandfather clock that wears spectacles, you could describe it as being *tick-tock-tocular*.

Many people wear glasses because they have one good eye and one weak eye. Such people could be called *sesquocular* (sĕs-KWŎK-yōō-lăr, from Latin: *sesqui*—one-and-a-half). Back in days of yore when monocles were all the rage, you could spot a sesquoculist a hundred yards away. But not anymore. Ever since eyeglasses and contact lenses came along to sweep monocles into oblivion, sesquoculism has gone—if you'll pardon the expression—out of sight. No longer can you tell just by looking whether someone has one good eye and one weak eye. Now you have to ask.

And you'd better ask with care. If a young man walks up to a lady at a party and says, "I hear you're sesquocular," he may get his face slapped.

Ducks who have one good eye and one weak eye can be called *sesquackular* (sĕs-QUĂK-yōō-lăr). But you seldom see a duck wearing eyeglasses because most ducks have trouble reading an eye chart.

---

*If you use the Latin root *sexus* (meaning "sex"), then sexocular fits anyone who has soft and dreamy "bedroom" eyes.

124 **quadocular**

quizbang

(KWĬZ-bang) noun.
A surprise test.
(*quiz*—etymology unknown; *bang* from Scandinavian: *banga*—to hammer)
Coined by Roland Drake, Toronto, Ontario.

> *Student:* "Sir, are we having a quizbang tomorrow?"
> *Teacher:* "If I tell you we're having a quizbang, it won't be a quizbang, will it? So you see, it's impossible for me to tell you."

Quizbangs keep students on their toes because they strike with the speed of a lightning bolt. And anything that strikes that fast deserves to be followed by an exclamation mark: *quizbang!*

But wait! Another punctuation mark is lurking in the shadows, just waiting for the chance to pop out at us. The exclamation mark at the end of *quizbang!* really only applies to the *bang!* Because a quiz is full of questions, it should also be full of question marks. Hence, *quizbang!* should be written *quiz?bang!*

If you think *quiz?bang!* looks funny, you could take plain old *quizbang* and follow it with an *interrobang*. That's the world's newest punctuation mark—a combined question mark (*interro*gative) and exclamation mark (*bang!*). It was designed in the United States for punctuating sentences that are both interrogative and exclamatory.

"How about that‽"

rexile

(RĔX-ĭl) noun.
The fate suffered by kings and queens who are deposed but not decapitated. Banished from the kingdom or "queendom," they are forced into *rexile*. Lesser mortals are merely exiled.
(Latin: *rex*—king; *exsilium*—banishment)
Coined by the author.

On January 30, 1649, the swing of an axe severed the head from the body of King Charles the First of England. Defeated at the hands of Oliver Cromwell in the English Civil War, Charles was a victim of regicide. If he had been *rexiled,* he might have had the good fortune to die of old age.

His son, James the Second, was luckier. Captured by the invading William of Orange in 1688, James was allowed to escape. After all, why kill him and stain the hands of the new King William with the blood of the former English monarch? James fled to France where he lived in rexile.

After Napoleon was defeated at the Battle of Waterloo in 1815, he was banished to a lonely island in the South Atlantic named St. Helena. If "the little Corsican" had been a royal-blooded king instead of a mere upstart emperor, his island home could have been renamed Rex Isle.

riggafrutch

(RĬG-ă-frŭch) expletive.
A perfectly clean swear word with a therapeutic value equal to or greater than any four-letter word yet invented.
(born out of spontaneous verbal combustion)
Coined by Bob Krueger, Toronto, Ontario.

Riggafrutch cannot be traced back to Latin, Greek, or any other language. Like the goddess Athene bursting in full armour from the head of Zeus, it emerged full-blown and fully formed from the vocal chords of Bob Krueger, a Toronto high school music teacher.

It all happened late one afternoon in the middle of a music rehearsal Krueger was conducting. One particular musical segment was posing a real challenge and had to be tackled over and over again. Krueger could feel his patience wearing thin, but—always a gentleman—he suppressed the urge to curse. Finally he could hold it back no longer: "Aw, riggafrutch! Let's try it again."

None of the students were shocked at his language because none of them had ever heard *riggafrutch* before. Neither had Krueger. But he felt much better for having said it.

You too can vent your spleen in mixed company without resorting to such vulgar, uncouth, and shocking obscenities as ___ or ___ ! or even (Heaven forbid!) ___ ! If you include the exclamation mark, the 11-letter *riggafrutch* gives you three times more vocal ammunition than any of the old worn-out four-letter curses. And with a tongue roll on the two r's, you can stretch out the verbal pleasure to a full half-minute of blowing off steam.

What a catharsis! Krueger should go into the patent medicine business. If *riggafrutch* can be bottled, he'll make a fortune.

> *Riggafrutchical*—adjective describing a conversation interspersed with frequent outbursts of "Riggafrutch!"
> *Riggafrutchemania*—excessive use of "Riggafrutch!"
> *Riggafrutchephobia*—fear of using "Riggafrutch!" in mixed company because some listeners (especially those who haven't read this book) may think it's a dirty word instead of a clean one. If you have riggafrutchephobic tendencies, you can banish your

128 riggafrutch

fears simply by carrying this book around with you. If anyone accuses you of foul language, just flip the book open to this entry.

Warning: If you swear on your deathbed, you'll soon come down with *riggafrutchemortis!*

sesquicousins

(SĔS-kwĭ-kŭz-ĭnz) noun.
Relatives who are first cousins and second cousins *simultaneously*!
(Latin: *sesqui*—one-and-a-half + *cousin*)
Coined by Margaret Pritchard, Toronto, Ontario, to describe a relationship within her family in which two brothers married two first cousins.

As soon as Margaret Pritchard telephoned me about *sesquicousin*, I suddenly realized the Sherk family was blessed with sesquicousinry! My father, Frank Sherk, and his cousin, Calvin Sherk, were first cousins through their mothers and second cousins through their fathers because two sisters married two first cousins:

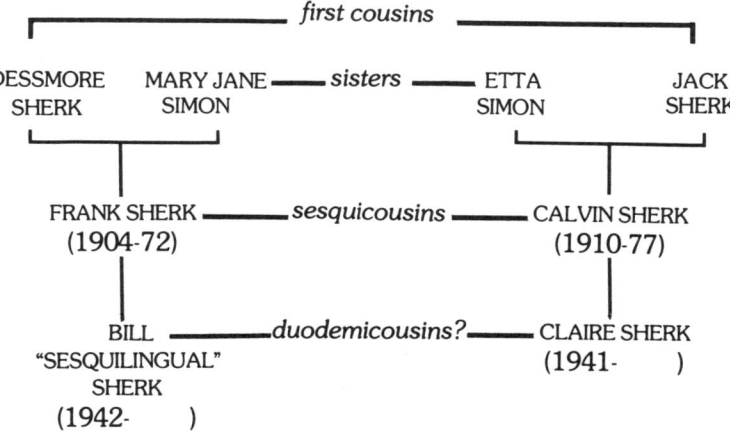

The two marriages that produced these sesquicousins took place around the turn of the century near Leamington in southwestern Ontario. This and similar arrangements were probably not unusual in rural areas in the late nineteenth century, when a person often married someone from a nearby farm.

Check your family tree right away. You might find a sesquiplenitude of sesquicousins! And if you find an odd family relationship for which no word exists, contact me *immediately*!!!

sesquidextrous

(sĕs-kwĭ-DĔX-trŭs) adjective.
Skilful with one hand and clumsy with the other. "I'm not ambidextrous. I'm *sesquidextrous!*"
(Latin: *sesqui*—one-and-a-half; *dexter*—right hand)
Coined by the author.

Another gaping hole in the English language has now been filled. How many times have you been asked if you're ambidextrous? And if you're not, you probably reply: "No, I'm not."

With *sesquidextrous* in your vocabulary, you can now stop telling people what you *aren't* and start telling them what you *are!*

Strictly speaking, you're sesquidextrous only if you are right-handed because *dexter* in Latin means *right hand*. But you lefties out there (and I'm one myself) are not going to be left out. We can call ourselves *sesquisinistrous* (sĕs-kwĭ-sĭ-NĬS-trŭs) from the Latin *sinister* meaning *left hand*.

Ambidexterity can be a great asset. But not everyone who has it is willing to admit it. In her Pulitzer Prize-winning novel, *To Kill a Mockingbird,* Harper Lee describes a rape trial in the courtroom of a small town in Alabama:

> Mr. Gilmer asked him one more question. "About your writing with your left hand, are you ambidextrous, Mr. Ewell?"
>
> "I most positively am not, I can use one hand good as the other. One hand good as the other," he added, glaring at the defense table.

Obviously, Mr. Ewell is not sesquidextrous—he's ambidextrous. But some people are neither of these because they're somewhere in between. On this very point, I received the following letter from Kenneth Hodges of Saskatoon, Saskatchewan:

> I should like to know whether or not there is a word for a person who is right handed for some activities but left handed for others and is unable to switch one to the other. "Ambidextrous" does not accurately describe such a person. If there is such a word, I should be pleased to know what it is. If not, perhaps you

sesquidextrous

can come up with one. I might say for example that I am right handed at tennis but left handed at golf.

I know of no such word so let's make one up right now: *duodextrous*. This word indicates that you have two (*duo*) hands that are skilful (*dextrous*) but are not necessarily both (*ambi*) suitable for the same activities. If you happen to be duodextrous and proud of it, you can take a tip from Batman and Robin and refer to your hands as the Dynamic Duo!

sesquigamist

(sĕs-KWĬG-ă-mĭst) noun.
A person once married and now engaged to be married again.
(Latin: *sesqui*—one-and-a-half; Greek: *gamos*—marriage)
Coined by Glenn Wong, Toronto, Ontario.

Are you planning to marry for the second time? If so, you are now living in a state of *sesquigamy*—a temporary condition, unless of course the engagement drags on and on and on. . . .

When you tie the knot for the second time, you become a deuterogamist (from Greek: *deuteros*—second). That's a word you can find in Webster's dictionary. Psychologist Murray Banks tells the story of the woman whose husband died and she inscribed on his tombstone: "My light has gone out." A few years later she was about to remarry. She asked the bishop if she should remove the inscription. He said, "Oh, no. Just add underneath: 'I have struck another match.' "

If you strike a second match while your first marriage is still burning, you'll be guilty of bigamy and in big trouble with the law. The law also frowns on polygamy (having several spouses) regardless of which form it takes: polygyny (having several wives, from Greek: *gyne*—woman) or polyandry (having several husbands, from Greek: *andros*—man). If you've always had a yen for multiple mates, there is a way you can have them all and still not break the law. You can be married to *dozens* of people as long as you marry and divorce them one at a time. This practice is known as serial monogamy. And if you court your spouse-to-be on a bicycle built for two, we could call it tandem monogamy. Either way, you'll be doing a lot of monogging!

But some people are never satisfied. William Cosmos Monkhouse once wrote about a fellow for whom one wife at a time was not enough:

> There once was an old man of Lyme
> Who married three wives at a time;
>   When asked "Why a third?"
>   He replied, "One's absurd!
> And bigamy, sir, is a crime "

sesquiguous

(sĕs-KWĬG-yōō-ŭs) adjective.
Having two possible meanings, one of which is far more likely than the other. In other words, anything which is only slightly ambiguous. (Latin: *sesqui*—one-and-a-half; + ambi*guous*)
Coined by Bill Weir, Toronto, Ontario.

Here is a classic example of *sesquiguity:*

"We're having a turkey for dinner tonight."

One of your dinner guests *might* be a turkey gobbler (especially during *Be Kind to Animals Week*) but the chances are overwhelmingly in favour of the turkey being on the menu, not on the guest list.

Would you like to have
YOUR NAME
in the next edition
of
BRAVE NEW WORDS?

It's easy! Just compose a few sesquiguous statements and send them in on the convenient word card at the back of this book. We'll publish a selection of them—along with the names of the contributors—*right on this page* in our next edition!

sesquilingual

(sĕs-kwĭ-LĬNG-gwăl) adjective.
Knowing one language and part of another. "I'm not bilingual. I'm *sesquilingual!*"
(Latin: *sesqui*—one-and-a-half; *lingua*—tongue)
Coined by the author.

Sesquilingual is the word that gave birth to this dictionary you are now reading. It all began with a conversation in front of Northern Secondary School in Toronto on a cold but sunny December morning in 1975. I was walking along the sidewalk with a friend and colleague named Bob Warren (we were both on the staff of Northern Secondary School at the time) and—just for fun—we began talking to one another in fractured French. Both of us had studied French all through high school but neither one of us was bilingual. We were somewhere in between.

Suddenly I stopped dead in my tracks! With sledgehammer impact I realized for the first time that the English language contained no word for a person who knows one language and part of another. Between *unilingual* and *bilingual* lay a vast empty linguistic chasm just begging to be filled.

What to fill it with was obvious. Both *uni* (one) and *bi* (two) have been borrowed from Latin and *sesqui* is the Latin prefix for one-and-a-half (as in *sesquicentennial*—150 years, or one-and-a-half centuries). I turned to Bob in a frenzy of excitement and screamed, "Guess what! We're *sesquilingual!*"

I quickly became convinced there must be other gaps in the English language just waiting for word coiners to come along and fill them up. With that thought in mind, I arranged for newspaper, radio, and television coverage to solicit new words to add to the ones I was now busily coining myself.

The result is this book. *Sesquilingual* is a very special entry because without it all these other new words might never have met one another.

And *sesquilingual* sounds *so* impressive. Nine times out of ten (and I'm speaking here from personal experience), if you tell people you're sesquilingual, they'll say, "My gosh! You mean you can speak *six* languages?"

sesquilingual

But it was one-and-a-half languages that John Fraser of the Toronto *Globe and Mail* had in mind when he reviewed the French play, *The Trojan War Will Not Take Place,* on May 6, 1977: "It is done in French, although the company provides a free earphone set that gives a fairly tortured running translation. If you're a 'sesquilingual' dummy like me, you'll find yourself leaving the set on only for the difficult longer speeches and gratefully turning it off when you can make your own language connections—or, more to the point, acting connections." Fraser put quotation marks around *sesquilingual* because he first saw the word a few days earlier in a letter I had written to the editor of *The Globe and Mail*. Fraser (who is now the *Globe*'s Peking correspondent) assures me that when he uses the word again, he will omit the quotation marks. By so doing, he will drive *sesquilingual* just that much deeper into the living heart of the English language.

If you're already bilingual, you can look back to the days when you were sesquilingual (unless of course you have two mother tongues—or one mother tongue and one father tongue). And if you want to stay bilingual, you should give your second language some regular exercise. Otherwise you'll slowly sink back into sesquilingualism.

There must be hundreds of millions of people throughout the world who are sesquilingual and don't even know what to call themselves. Until now, they have had no word to accurately describe their linguistic status.

Oxford and Webster, take note!

sesquiphonic

(sĕs-kwĭ-FŎN-ĭk) adjective.
Having a sound followed by an echo.
(Latin: *sesqui*—one-and-a-half; Greek: *phone*—sound)
Coined by John Calvin, Toronto, Ontario.

John Calvin's new word will be a big hit with every disc jockey who broadcasts from an echo chamber.

sesquisuit

(SĔS-kwĭ-sōōt) noun.
A suit with a reversible jacket.
(Latin: *sesqui*—one-and-a-half + *suit*)
Coined by Michael Granatstein, Toronto, Ontario.

The sesquisuit should be in the wardrobe of every dashing gentleman- or lady-about-town. When the office clock hits 5 P.M., you can peel off your conservative business jacket, pull it inside-out, slip into a flashy layer of threads, and sally forth to the nearest dinner party.

Of course, if you want the office staff to think you have *two* jackets instead of one, you'll have to perform a surreptitious switcheroo—which is no great inconvenience when you consider your sartorial splendour is only a broom closet away.

sexophile

(SĔX-ō-fīl) noun.
A person who enjoys sex as an integral part of a warm and intimate relationship.
(Latin: *sexus*—sex; Greek: *philein*—to love)
Coined by the author in April 1976 for a Conference on Sexuality at York University, Toronto, Ontario.

Are you a *sexophile*?

The English language abounds with words full of love: *philatelist* (lover of stamps), *philosopher* (lover of wisdom), *philanthropist* (lover of mankind), *philologist* (lover of words), and *bibliophile* (lover of books). But what word can you find in your dictionary for a person who loves sex?

Oh, you'll find *nymphomania,* but that describes a condition that most people consider abnormal and it only applies to females (the male version is *satyromania*). For the person, male or female, who thoroughly enjoys sex as an integral part of a warm and intimate relationship, our language is strangely silent.

That silence can now be shattered with *sexophile*—a word which, appropriately enough, is the offspring of a union between two classical languages: Latin and Greek (see etymology above).

In his bestselling book, *The Joy of Sex,* Alex Comfort presents a gourmet's guide to lovemaking. If you're a gourmet where wine is concerned, you can call yourself an oenophilist. And now, if you're a gourmet where sex is concerned, you can call yourself a sexophile.

Oxford and Webster, make room for it! You can squeeze *sexophile* in somewhere between *sexlocular* and *sexpartite*.

> *Special note:* If *sexophile* sounds too blatantly *sexy* for your tender ears (the accent falls on *sex*), try *sexophilist* (sĕx-ŎF-ĭl-ĭst). But be careful how you use it. *Sexophilist,* with a slightly different spelling, describes a person who doesn't like sex at all: *sexawful*ist

Sex is not always what it appears to be. The Latin root *sexus* means "sex" but the Latin root *sex* means "six" as in *sextet* (a group of six musicians). But it's not easy to get away from *s-e-x*, as Maxwell

sexophile

Nurnberg and Morris Rosenblum point out in *How To Build A Better Vocabulary*:

> And what is the word for someone in his sixties? We'll let Helen Westley, veteran Theater Guild actress, answer that one. While she was working on a set in Hollywood, an extra gushed up to her.
>
> "Why, Miss Westley, what are *you* doing in this picture?"
>
> "My dear, haven't you heard," replied Miss Westley, "I furnish the sexagenarian appeal."

sherkquacious

(shŭr-KWĀ-shŭs) adjective.
Speaking or writing with flamboyant words and phrases. A style characteristic of Bill "Sesquilingual" Sherk who, for example, promotes a local variety show with sherkquacious bombast: "This star-studded musical extravaganza comes but once every two years for a one-night stand and always leaves the audience screaming for more!!! And the best part is the price: not $300, not $30, but only $3 a ticket!!!"
(eponym based on *Sherk* + *loquacious* from Latin: *loquax*—talkative)
Coined by Canadian poet John Robert Colombo, Toronto, Ontario.

When John Robert Colombo coined *sherkquacious*, he turned Yours Truly into an eponym (a word based on someone's name). I then picked up where he left off and soon discovered that if I added the right prefixes and suffixes, I could scatter my surname all over the world:

> *Sherkshire*—a tiny, independent kingdom in the heart of England, just west of Berkshire (BĂRK-shŭr). It doesn't appear on any maps because the British are too embarrassed to admit they've never been able to conquer it.
> *Sherkwood Forest*—the home of Robin Hood. It was here that Mr. Hood was pursued by the Sherkiff of Nottingham.
> *Sherkopolis*—(shŭr-KŎP-ŏ-lĭs)—An ancient Greek city-state temporarily enslaved by the Persian king, Sherkus the Great.
> *Sherkcaster* (SHŬR-kă-stŭr)—A Roman military outpost in the Swiss Alps. Hannibal flattened it when he passed through with his elephants in 218 B.C..
> *Sherkistan*—a tiny panjandrumate straddling the border between Afghanistan and Baluchistan. Currently ruled by Sherkindi the Invisible.
> *McSherks*—a clan of Scottish Sherks who re-named the Firth of Forth the Ferk of Sherk.

sherkquacious

O'Sherks—a group of Irish Sherks who, after the failure of their potato crop, migrated to Sherksylvania (now called Pennsylvania) in the 1670s. Another group, in search of bigger potatoes, pushed further west and settled in Sherkaho (later renamed Idaho).

Sherkston—a tiny Ontario hamlet on the north shore of Lake Erie about 20 miles west of Buffalo, New York. Named after the Sherks who settled here as United Empire Loyalists following the American Revolutionary War. Unlike the other places listed above, Sherkston is authentic. It even has its own post office!

As indicated above, *sherkquacious* is a combination of *Sherk* and *loquacious*. *Roget's Thesaurus* puts *loquacious* in the same company as *talkative, garrulous, chattering, chatty, declamatory, fluent, voluble, effusive, glib,* and *flippant*.

But what about those people at the other extreme—the strong, silent types? Roget gives us *taciturn, laconic, concise, sententious, close, close-mouthed, curt, reserved,* and *reticent*. And of all these synonyms, *laconic* is the only one you can find on a map. It comes from Laconia, an area in southern Greece where the tight-lipped ancient Spartans lived.

Because they were obsessed with maintaining a military state, the Spartans paid scant attention to literature or the arts. So sparing were they in the use of words that the name of their homeland entered the English language as a synonym for *terse*. In *Word Power Made Easy*, Norman Lewis provides a classic example of Spartan brevity:

> Legend has it that when Philip of Macedonia was storming the gates of Sparta (or Laconia), he sent a message to the besieged king saying, "If we capture your city we will burn it to the ground."
>
> A one-word answer came back: "If."

One of the most laconic of American presidents was Calvin Coolidge (1923-1929), who firmly believed that if you don't say anything, you can't be called upon to repeat it. (No wonder he was nicknamed "Cautious Cal.") According to Norman Lewis:

> A young newspaperwoman was sitting next to Coolidge at a

banquet, so the story goes, and turned to him mischievously.

"Mr. Coolidge," she said, "I have a bet with my editor that I can get you to say more than two words to me this evening."

"*You lose*," Coolidge rejoined simply.

And so we see that the ancient Spartans (and at least one American president) practised restraint in the use of words. But the Spartans failed to exercise the same restraint when it came to sex:

> In Sparta, celibacy was a crime. Street gangs of women beat up bachelors. Unmarried men and girls might be thrust into the same dark room, where all groped for mates. Spartans, wrote Plutarch, "sometimes had children by their wives before ever they saw their faces by daylight." [National Geographic Society, *Greece and Rome—Builders of Our World*]

If "Cautious Cal" had been King of Sparta, those lecherous Laconians would have been chaste—or chased out of town.

siberbia

(sī-BŬR-bē-ă) noun.
A new, improved synonym for *suburbia*.
(contraction of *Siberia* and *suburbia*)
Coined by Lynn McMurray while teaching a class of Urban Studies at North Toronto Collegiate, Toronto, Ontario.

If you have ever lived in the suburbs and felt isolated from the heart of the city, *siberbia* is the word you've been waiting for. The suburban housewife stranded at home without a car knows how it feels to be exiled to Siberia.

Besides, the word *suburbs* is not as good as you might think it is. It has impeccable Latin credentials (*sub*—under; *urbs*—city) but therein lies the problem. Suburbanites do not live *under* a city, they live *around* it. The only true *sub*urbanites are moles and worms and occupants of basement apartments. Back in ancient Rome it was a different story. The suburbs of Rome really were *sub*urbs. Rome itself was built on the famous Seven Hills of Rome and so the outskirts of the city were below (or *under*) the level of the city itself.

By changing *suburbia* to *siberbia*, you might think we are cutting this word off from its Roman origins—but in point of fact we are not. Siberia is a vast, isolated suburb into which many people have been exiled. The government in Moscow has sent them there. And the city of Moscow regards itself as another Rome. When the Roman Empire fell in the West in the fifth century A.D., the imperial torch was passed to Byzantium (Constantinople) which became the second Rome for another thousand years. When it was overrun by the Turks in 1453, a third Rome sprang up in the north. According to the authors of *The Foundations of the West,* "Moscow became the new headquarters of the Orthodox Church, the Patriarch of Moscow taking up the task of the Patriarch of Constantinople. Ivan the Great, Czar of Russia, married the niece of the last Byzantine Emperor and claimed his power, adopting the Byzantine eagle as his own coat-of-arms. These heirs of autocracy and Orthodoxy went so far as to state, in the sixteenth century, 'Two Romes have fallen, and the third stands, and a fourth there shall not be.' "

And so, no matter how you look at it, *siberbia* is a winner. And it is helping to perpetuate a fine tradition. By taking two old words and slamming them together to make a new one, Lynn McMurray is following in the footsteps of Lewis Carroll (1832-1898), author of *Alice in Wonderland,* who coined such gems as *chortle* (from chuckle and snort), *galumph* (from gallop and thump), *mimsy* (from miserable and flimsy), and *slithy* (from lithe and slimy). Because, as Carroll pointed out, "there are two meanings packed up in one word," he called such words portmanteau words (a portmanteau is a suitcase with two compartments hinged together).

Such words are also called blend words. Familiar blendings include *brunch, smog,* and *motel.* But the real estate agency that advertised a *splanch* for sale (a split-level ranch-style home) was probably barking up the wrong tree. Who would want to live in a splanch?

sinistrologist

(sĭn-ĭ-STRŎL-ŏ-jĭst) noun.
A person who studies left-handed people.
(Latin: *sinister*—on the left hand; Greek: *logos*—the study of)
Coined by Lawrie Weiser, sinistrologist extraordinaire and proprietor of The Sinister Shoppe, Toronto, Ontario.

The English language is far more flattering to right-handers than it is to left-handers. From the French *droit* we have the English *adroit* (ă-DROYT), meaning skilful or resourceful. From the Latin *dexter* we have *dexterity*, meaning physical or mental skill.

But when we switch to the left hand, the lefties of the world get a linguistic slap in the face. In addition to meaning left, the French *gauche* also means clumsy and awkward, and it is this meaning of the word that has entered English, especially in a social sense: "Don't be so gauche! You should never ask a lady her age!"

The Latin root has become even more insulting. *Sinister* now means evil-looking or threatening. But why? The answer can be found in a fascinating little book called *The Left-hander's World* by Alvin and Barbara Silverstein: "In the days when running water and effective soaps were not available, it would be very unhealthy to place a hand in the family's food after it had been soiled by attending to toilet functions. The problem was solved (in the Middle East) by assigning strict roles to the two hands: one would be used for eating and other 'clean' tasks, and the other would be used only for the necessary but unclean functions. As anthropologist Randy Kandel phrases it, in such societies 'you eat with your right and wipe your bottom with your left.'"

In ancient Rome, putting your best foot forward and putting your right foot forward amounted to the same thing. Many wealthy Roman households had a servant stationed at the front door to make sure all visitors entered with the right foot first.

At the Roman Coliseum, the difference between left and right sometimes meant the difference between life and death. Gladiators were often given special instructions on how to grapple with a left-handed opponent, whose most important weapon was the element of surprise.

145

sinistrologist

Grappling of a different sort sometimes becomes a problem with a little South American fish known as the anableps. Silverstein and Silverstein explain why: "Each female anableps has a sexual opening only on one side of her body, either the right or the left. The male anableps has a single sexual organ, either on the right or on the left. A pair of anableps that are both right-handed (dextral) or both left-handed (sinistral) cannot mate at all—they simply do not fit together. Fortunately, both males and females are about evenly divided, half dextral and half sinistral, so all have good chances of finding a mate."

Despite centuries of effort by right-handers to "correct" lefties, the pages of history are filled with famous and infamous people who figured that, for themselves at least, right was wrong and left was right. Among them: Alexander the Great, Charlemagne ("Big Chuck"), Leonardo da Vinci, Lord Nelson, Billy the Kid, Jack the Ripper, King George VI, Cole Porter, Babe Ruth, Harry S. Truman, Charlie Chaplin, Judy Garland, Betty Grable, and Marilyn Monroe.

Famous lefties still living include Beatles Paul McCartney and Ringo Starr, Carol Burnett, Jack Carter, Richard Dreyfuss, Peter Fonda, Gerald Ford, Rock Hudson, Danny Kaye, Cloris Leachman, Kim Novak, Ryan O'Neal, Arnold Palmer, Ronald Reagan, Robert Redford, Don Rickles, Terry Thomas, Dick Van Dyke, and Paul Williams. And thanks to astronaut Wally Schirra, a lefty has gone to the moon and back.

Left-handers now have several specialty shops across North America which cater to their particular needs. One of these sinistral emporiums (or, if you prefer, *emporia*) is The Sinister Shoppe operated by Lawrie Weiser at 71 McCaul Street in the Village by the Grange in Toronto. Weiser is quick to point out that in his shop, "the customer is seldom right." And although Weiser himself stands upright (up*left*?), his sales catalogue definitely leans to the left. Under "Gadgets for the Gauche Gourmet" you can find left-handed pie servers, oven mitts, corkscrews, carving knives, soup ladles, measuring cups, and can openers. For left-handed sports buffs you can order left-handed tennis gloves or golf-gloves and copies of *Left-handed Golf* by Bob Charles, left-handed winner of the British Open. Weiser's T-shirts will fit anyone who has two arms, a neck, and a torso—but only lefties can wear them "correct"-side-out.

#A63 is Weiser's trademark—an illustrated southpaw. Lefties have

been called southpaws since 1891 when the term first appeared in a Chicago newspaper. It originated in a baseball park on Chicago's West Side. The pitcher's mound faced west and so a left-handed pitcher had to use his "south paw." Probably no one at the time thought this new word would catch on—but catch on it did! And if *southpaw* could pitch itself into the dictionary, there's hope yet for all the entries in *Brave New Words*.

Northpaw, anyone?

slantendicularist

(slănt-ĕn-DĬK-yōō-lăr-ĭst) noun.
An artist who hangs his paintings at a slant to capture the attention of prospective buyers.
(*slant* + *perpendicular* + *ist*. *Webster's Dictionary* includes *slantendicular* ["a slanted line"] but only *Brave New Words* gives you *slantendicularist*.)
Coined by the author following a suggestion by his aunt, Florence Beautenmiller, Royal Oak, Michigan.

Hang your paintings at a slant and you'll put yourself one step ahead of the competition. You might need that extra step, especially if you're flogging your masterpieces at a really big art sale in competition with hundreds of other canvases.

Amateur or fly-by-night slantendicularists will find their paintings remain at a slant only until an orthomuralist—a compulsive picture-straightener—comes on the scene. Those artists who are true devotees of slantendicularism protect themselves from the threat of orthomuralistic sabotage by giving their paintings a *permanent* slant.

slantendicularist

There are two ways to do this: Paint a picture of the Leaning Tower of Pisa *or* cleverly install across the bottom edge of each picture frame a sealed tube with a heavy ball bearing inside. If someone straightens the picture, it won't stay that way for long.

If, despite the slant, your paintings don't sell, you can resort to double-barrelled slantendicularism by attaching each painting to the pendulum of a cuckoo clock.

If they still don't sell, you should then use the method that *never fails* to attract attention: a self-destructing picture hook which allows each painting to fall with a crash to the floor whenever three or more people are standing nearby.

And if your paintings *still* don't sell (broken frames and all), buy yourself a ladder and pick-up truck and start painting with a roller instead of a brush.

Special note: If you're looking for the *artist* in *slantendicularist,* just yank out the *t* from between *n* and *e* and squeeze it in between *r* and *i.*

spork

(spork) noun.
A spoon with fork prongs at the tip. Available in plastic at fast-food outlets.
(contraction of *spoon* and *fork,* from Old English: *spon*—a spoon; *forca*—a fork)
Coined by Desmond Ottley, Mississauga, Ontario.

With fast-food outlets sprouting faster than you can say "Kentucky fried chicken," the plastic spork is here to stay. Why supply your customers with three eating utensils when you can now do the job with only two? Separate spoons and forks are now on the way out, the latest victims of rising costs and shrinking profits. Even farmers may find they have to trade in their pitchforks for supersporks so they can pitch hay and shovel manure at the same time. The day may come when the only fork around will be the fork in the road.

The spork should not be confused with the *foon,* an eating utensil with a fork at one end and a spoon at the other. During a typical meal, the foon must be frequently twirled around according to the order of dishes—one way for salad, the other way for soup, one way for meat and potatoes, the other way for stirring your coffee, then back again

for a slice of apple pie. The foon is obviously the ideal gift for a majorette who likes to practise her baton-twirling during dinner.

And *foon* should have no trouble at all in slipping into the English language. Any word that rhymes with *tycoon, typhoon,* and *buffoon* can't miss!

swinephone

(SWĪN-ĕ-fōn) noun.
A person who speaks pig Latin.
(Old English: *swin*—swine; Greek: *phone*—sound)
Coined by Gene Taylor, Canadian television talk show host, Toronto, Ontario.

Contrary to what you may think, Gene Taylor's new word is not designed for a short-legged mammal with cloven hoofs, bristly hair, and a cartilaginous snout. *Swinephone* is the exclusive property of human beings who speak pig Latin, which the *Heritage International Dictionary* defines as, "a coded jargon in which the initial consonant of each word is transposed to the end of that word with -*ay* (ā) added to form a new syllable, as *igpay atinlay* for *pig Latin*."

But it's only a matter of time before Taylor's neologism is extended to include someone who hogs the telephone.

A close cousin to *swinephone* in more ways than one is *frankophone,* coined by Bill O'Connell of Armdale, Nova Scotia. A frankophone is a telephone shaped like a hot dog in case you want to chew out your caller or you get hungry on a long-distance call.

tapotheque

(TĀP-ō-tĕk) noun.
A discotheque that plays tapes instead of records.
(*tape* + French: *bibliothèque*—a library)
Coined by Don Burnett, Charlottetown, Prince Edward Island.

Most discotheques are really tapotheques because they play tapes instead of records. And with good reason. If the music comes from records, the needle might start jumping around as soon as everyone gets out on the dance floor.
But if the tapes start jumping, take out extra life insurance fast! You're in an earthquake zone.
Both *discotheque* and *tapotheque* are offshoots of *bibliothèque*, the French word for *library*. One can easily imagine other offshoots:

>*antiquetheque*—library of books on buying, selling, and restoring antique furniture
>*autotheque*—library of fix-it manuals for the family car (usually housed on shelves in the garage)
>*cylindrotheque*—library of wax cylinders for gramophones
>*phototheque*—a photo library
>*pornotheque*—library of pornographic literature
>*subterratheque*—an underground library
>*teethotheque*—library of medical books at dental college
>*teetotaltheque*—library of books on alcohol abuse
>*trashotheque*—library of trashy dime-store novels or library of books on garbage disposal

Brave New Words now offers you a free lesson in disco dancing *at no extra charge!* The *U-turn* (shown on the next page) can be danced singly or in couples. It has eight beats and then repeats. Start with both feet side by side. For dancing the U-turn in couples, both partners face each other, man with right arm around woman's waist and left hand holding woman's right. Footwork same for both.

154 tapotheque

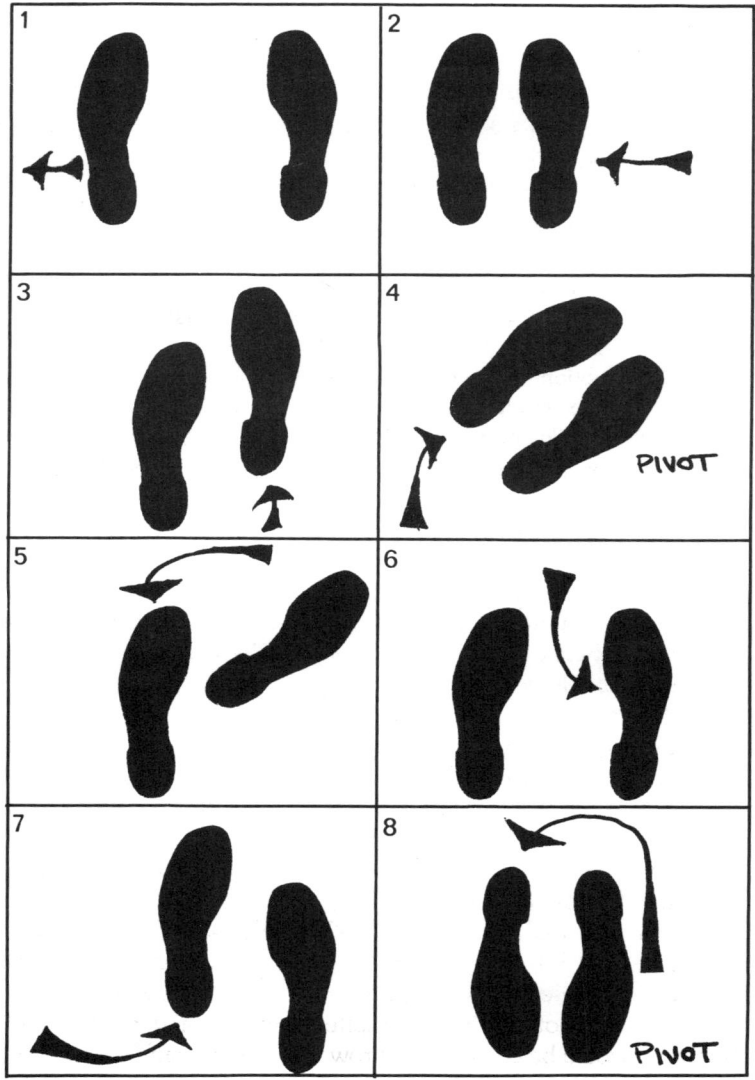

threek

(thrēk) noun.
A four-pronged fork with one prong gone. "Waiter! You've given me a threek! I asked for a fork."
(*three* + *fork* from Old English: *forca*—a fork)
Coined by David Axelrad, Willowdale, Ontario.

According to Professor Loof Lirpa (a notoriously unreliable source of information who always spells his name backwards), the fork was first invented in the English county of Norsex in the year 1144. A monk in a Norsexian monastery had stumbled upon the word *fourkk* in an old Anglo-Saxon manuscript but had no idea what it meant. Later that day, while eating with his fingers in a nearby inn, this same monk passed on the mysterious word to a local tinsmith of Roman ancestry named Prongus Bendus. Prongus was intrigued with *fourkk* and promised the monk he would try to turn the word to some useful purpose.

Returning to his shop that evening, Prongus fashioned each letter out of tin and mounted FOURKK on the wall over his workbench. He stared at the letters a long time, then climbed the stairs to his humble bedchamber above the shop.

Late that night, while England slept, inspiration struck! In the middle of a snore, Prongus bounded from his bed and dashed downstairs with a spluttering candle clutched in his hand. In the flickering gloom he made his way over to his workbench, above which the tin letters of FOURKK glowed in the dark like ghostly sentinels.

He removed the letter *U* from the wall and straightened it out to form a handle. He then removed the second *K* and bent its four prongs around to make them parallel, then he attached the prongs to the handle and "Eureka!" A superbly-crafted instrument for guiding food from your plate into your mouth. Sticky fingers, farewell!

Prongus then noticed the four letters still hanging on the wall: F-O-R-K. "It would be a shame to throw these letters out," he thought. "Maybe I can find a use for them too . . ."

tonguetipitis

(tŭng-tĭ-PIGHT-ĭs) noun.
The feeling you get when a word is stuck on the tip of your tongue. (Old English: *tunge*—tongue + *tip* + *itis* [inflammation]—the hot flush of embarrassment that leaps to your cheeks when you find yourself at a loss for words)
Coined by the author.

Tonguetipitis can save you from social embarrassment. The next time you're talking to someone and your mind goes blank, put your hand to your mouth and say: "Oh! I can't say another word. I've just come down with a sudden attack of tonguetipitis."

The person you're talking to will then say: "That sounds very painful. Listen, don't say another word. I'll do all the talking."

Now you can grab a few seconds—or even minutes—to collect your thoughts and figure out what to say next. When you're ready, simply say: "Well, I feel much better now. The attack seems to have passed. Now, as I was saying . . ."

According to John Cargill of Toronto, Ontario, tonguetipitis can be cured by drinking a generous quantity of boiled thesaurus leaves. Just toss a copy of *Roget's Thesaurus* (hard or soft cover) into a pot of boiling water, add a dash of hot mustard, let simmer for 20 minutes, then drink the whole pulpy scalding mess in one big gulp.

Almost immediately, a red-hot torrent of synonyms and antonyms will come belching out of your mouth. It's a good idea, when drinking this concoction, to have a fire extinguisher handy.

The famous *Roget's Thesaurus* of synonyms and antonyms (from Greek: *thesauros*—a treasure-house) was begun by an English scholar, physician, and incurable word lover named Peter Mark Roget (1779-1869). With such a wealth of words at his fingertips, Roget must have been quite a hit with the ladies. Poet John Robert Colombo imagines what he might have said on his first date:

ROGET'S GIRL
Let me peer into your eyes, orbs, blinkers, corneas,
    oculars, irises, peepers, etc.

tonguetipitis

Let me take a gander at your legs, limbs, stems, shanks, thighs, calves, gams, etc.
Let me catch a glimpse of your breasts, bustline, bosoms, boobs, tits, teats, duggs, etc.
Let me command a view of your behind, bottom, posterior, bum, butt, ass end, south end, etc.
Let me command a view of your, catch a glimpse of your, take a gander at your, peer into your *et cetera*.

ugloo

(ŬG-lōō) noun.
An ugly igloo.
(*ugly* from Old Norse: *uggr*—fear; Eskimo: *igloo*—igloo)
Coined by Hanns Skoutajan, Toronto, Ontario.

Every summer, more and more tourists are flocking into the Arctic to spend their holidays. And as they debouch from their plane somewhere inside the Arctic Circle, the first thought that springs to mind often is: "Let's build an igloo!"

But all too often the igloo turns into an *ugloo*—a grotesque assortment of ice blocks obviously fashioned by a rank amateur. If you want to end up with an igloo instead of an ugloo, hire a local *iglootect* (someone trained in *iglootecture*) to draw some plans for you. Then if you like the way your igloo turns out, you can subdivide a piece of tundra and start building them by the dozens—or even hundreds! Add a shopping plaza carved out of ice and presto—you've created an *igloopolis*.

If you build your igloo on one of the Arctic Islands, it might melt because, etymologically speaking, you are *almost* standing on a sun-drenched Greek isle in the middle of the Aegean Sea. The Arctic Islands are also called the Arctic Archipelago (from Greek: *archi*—chief, and *pelagos*—the sea). The chief sea for the ancient Greeks was the Aegean—and because the Aegean is dotted with islands, the word *archipelago* now refers to any large cluster of islands.

But how did the Aegean Sea get its name? Back in the legendary annals of Greek history lived Aegeus, King of Athens. Every year in those times, seven youths and seven maidens from Athens had to be sacrificed to the flesh-eating Minotaur, a half-man/half-bull that lived in a labyrinth under the palace of Knossos on the island of Crete. Theseus, son of Aegeus, had been selected as one of the victims.

Determined to slay the beast, Theseus told his father that the boat taking him to Crete would return to Athens flying a white sail if he were coming home alive and a black sail if he were dead.

As luck would have it, Theseus succeeded in killing the Minotaur but was in such a hurry to return home that he forgot to change the black sail for a white one. His father, watching from a cliff, saw the ship appear on the horizon with a black sail. Overcome with grief, he threw himself into the sea and drowned. Ever since, that sea has been called the Aegean.

Theseus, now fatherless, emerges as the tragic hero of the tale while the Minotaur is clearly the villain. This strange beast was, according to one version of the legend, the son of Europa, a beautiful Phoenician princess who had been abducted by Zeus in the form of a bull who swam with her to the island of Crete. The *-taur* in *minotaur* comes from the Greek *tauros,* a bull.

Another animal with four letters beginning with *b* is *bear,* and this is the animal that takes us back to the Arctic. The Greek word for bear is *arktos* and this word has been applied to the polar regions because the constellation of the Great Bear (Ursa Major) is in the northern heavens. The ancient Greeks so named it, probably not realizing that polar bears actually lived in the Arctic.

The ancient Greeks were no doubt equally unaware of the existence of Teddy bears. According to *Time* (Dec. 5, 1969): "The name was attached to a new line of stuffed bruins manufactured by the forerunner of the Ideal Toy Corp. and by Germany's Steiff Co. after President Theodore Roosevelt, on an expedition to Mississippi in 1902, refused to shoot a bear cub. Washington *Star* cartoonist Clifford Berryman instantly made the cub a symbol for Roosevelt, and the country went for the notion lock, stock, and bear jokes. (If T.R. is President when he is fully dressed, went one kneeslapper, what is he with his clothes off? Answer: Teddy bare.)"

Lovers of little stuffed bruins will lumber with delight through the pages of *Bear with Me,* an ursine classic written by British character actor Peter Bull. Bull's enthusiasm for Teddy bears is undeniable and unquenchable. He writes: "They have gone into battle on guns, tanks and in haversacks. They have saved lives by intercepting bullets, breaking falls, and just being around. They've flown around the world, been drowned in floods, burned in concentration camps and worshiped as totems. There are no cases of disloyal, treacherous or cowardly Teddy bears. They seem destined to survive everything and emerge as a triumphant symbol of something or other."

Bull himself owns fourteen Teddy bears. If he ever travels to the Arctic to build an ugloo or an igloo, you can bet he won't go there alone.

umbrellabat

(ŭm-BRĔL-ă-băt) noun.
A person who rings doorbells with the tip of his umbrella.
(Italian: *ombrella*—a shade + acro*bat* from Greek: *akrobatein*—to walk on tiptoe)
Coined by the author.

Take one umbrella, add the skill of an acrobat, mix well with a young man's natural urge to impress his girl friend and *voilà!* You have an *umbrellabat*.

Gene Taylor, Canadian television talk show host, has never forgotten his first fling with umbrellabatics. Anxious to impress his lady friend on the way to a house party, he waited till they reached the front door, then took careful aim, flicked his umbrella into the air, and delivered a rapier-like thrust toward the doorbell. He missed (when you miss, you're known as an *umbrellabotch*) and struck stucco instead. A big chunk of plaster fell to the ground.

His girl friend was not impressed.

unikini

(YOO-nĭ-kē-nē) noun.
A topless bikini *or* a skimpy pair of male trunks.
(Latin: *unus*—one + bi*kini*)
Coined by Atila Csanti, Toronto, Ontario.

In 1946, the United States conducted a series of tests of the atomic bomb on Bikini, a tiny coral island in the Pacific Ocean. But these atomic explosions were nothing compared to the anatomic impact of the first bikini bathing suits. And that's why they were called bikinis. They were named after the island. So if you thought the *bi* in bikini came from the Latin prefix *bi* for *two*, guess again.

In 1964, a San Francisco dancer named Carol Dada decided to go topless. Almost immediately, she became an international celebrity—and launched a topless craze unparalleled since the days of the bare-bosomed snake goddesses of ancient Crete. Carol Dada was now dancing in a unikini!

But this new word is not the exclusive property of showgirls. It can also be used by men who wear skimpy trunks. After a frenzied night of dancing at the local discotheque in *Saturday Night Fever,* John Travolta wakes up the next morning in wide-screen technicolour wearing nothing but a black unikini. Pajama salesmen are probably starving to death by now.

volnic

(VŎL-nĭk) noun.
An imaginary part of an automobile carburetor that can only be adjusted with a gafahvitz.
(etymology obscure)
Coined and used regularly by Bill O'Connell, Armdale, Nova Scotia.

O'Connell explains how he is able to use *volnic* and *gafahvitz* with astonishing frequency: "I travel a lot and I often run across females whose cars won't go. I check it out—gas, spark, ignition wires—and usually get it going. Then as I wipe my hands, I *calmly* announce to the grateful lass that I simply adjusted the volnic with my gafahvitz—and 99 times out of 100 she believes me! I can just *see* her telling somebody about this when she gets home."

But in this age of sexual equality, with more and more women enrolling in auto mechanics courses, O'Connell may soon meet his come-uppance. If *his* car breaks down at the side of the road and he can't fix it, a sympathetic female might stop to help him out. And after she gets it going, she might calmly announce, "Oh, it was nothing really. I simply adjusted the snickersnee with my gunkimeter."

willectomy

(wĭl-ĔK-tō-mē) noun.
The cutting from a will of someone who expects to receive an inheritance. Lawyer to relative of deceased: "I'm sorry, Mr. Farquhar, but your rich uncle has willectomized you."
(Old English: *willan*—will; Greek: *tome*—a cutting)
Coined by the author.

As a new word, *willectomy* is a poet's delight! It rhymes with *appendectomy, tonsillectomy, hysterectomy,* and *vasectomy.* That's worth at least five stanzas right there!

And *willectomy* may catch on in legal circles as well, especially if it applies to a whole family. For example, across-the-board willectomies result from any Last Will and Testament that begins: "I, being of sound mind, spent all my money while I was alive."

Equally sensible but far more difficult to arrange is the sentiment overheard one day near a Toronto cemetery: "If I can't take it with me, I'm not going."

Speaking of wills, any lawyer will tell you you should have one. But why don't people also have *won'ts*? A won't is a will in which you say what you *won't* do with your estate (". . . and my shiftless, no-good brother-in-law *won't* get one red cent.").

Xian

(ĔX-ē-ăn) noun.
A passive and indifferent Christian.
(*X* in place of *Christ,* probably inspired by the *X* in *Xmas*)
Coined by Canadian poet Irving Layton, Montreal, Quebec.

In the foreword of his recent book, *The Covenant,* Irving Layton explains why he coined this new word: "To discriminate the Christians who risked their lives for their faith from the passive and indifferent who did not I have decided to call the latter 'Xians' and their religion 'Xianity.'"

As a lexicographer, I am thrilled beyond compare that Irving Layton coined *Xian* because new words beginning with *X* are mighty difficult to find! *The Heritage Illustrated Dictionary* has only two pages of *X* words (compared to 168 pages for *S* words). Even *Y* and *Z* can only muster a measly 11 pages between them. It's as if the alphabet runs out of steam after it passes *W*.

Incidentally, *W* sounds a trifle redundant because it literally means *double U* and looks like it too. We couldn't call it *U-U* because that sounds too much like *yo-yo* and the letter *W* goes up and down enough already.

Strangely enough, the letter *X* by itself crops up far more often than those words that begin with *X*. We see the letter *X* everywhere—on clock faces using Roman numerals, on pedestrian crossings, at the end of love letters, and even on ladies' undergarments (remember the brassière ad on television telling you to "cross your heart"?).

The *X* section in *The Heritage Dictionary* takes you all the way from *xanthate* ("a salt of a xanthic acid"—wow!) to *xyster* ("a surgical instrument for scraping bones"—ouch!). One of the more interesting entries in between is this one: "*Xanthippe* (zăn-TĬP-ē)—the wife of Socrates, the Greek philosopher; proverbial as a shrewish and scolding woman."

If Xanthippe was so bitchy (Hey! That rhymes!), no wonder Socrates drank the hemlock that ended his life. Of course, Xanthippe might have gotten that way because of Socrates himself. He was *always* asking questions. And if *she* asked *him* a question, he probably—in true philosophic fashion—never gave her a straight answer.

yawnee

(yŏn-EE) noun.
A person who yawns after seeing someone else yawn.
(Old English: *geonian*—yawn + *ee*)
Coined by the author.

Can you look at this picture without yawning? I can't. In fact, I'm yawning so much I can hardly . . . (yawn) . . . finish writing this . . . (yawn) . . . page.

166 yawnee

Never underestimate the power of a yawn. A badly timed yawn can crush a budding romance: "Darling, I . . . (yawn) . . . love you."

And a single yawn can ruin a great party. It can trigger off an epidemic of yawning (a *yawnidemic?*) and send everyone off home to bed.

If you're writing a stage play, don't—and I repeat, don't—write a yawn into the script. If you do, the whole audience may start yawning—and that could spoil your chances for getting good reviews: "Don't bother going to see it. It's a crashing bore. Everyone was yawning."

As you can see, we're nearly at the end of *Brave New Words,* Volume One. And if *yawnee* does nothing else, it should convince you that word coining can be easy. Just take an existing word (preferably a verb) and add *ee.* For example:

> *burnee*—a person burned at the stake for witchcraft or heresy (used in a lecture on seventeenth century England by Professor Elliot Rose, University of Toronto)
> *choppee*—a victim of the guillotine in the French Revolution
> *snoree*—a person awakened by someone snoring
> *spongee*—a person who's an easy mark for spongers and freeloaders
> *usurpee*—a king or queen who loses his or her throne (King James II was usurpeed when William of Orange invaded England in 1688)

zedwyexian   zeewyexian

(Canadian spelling)   (American spelling)
(zēd-wī-ĔX-ē-ăn) noun.   (zē-wī-ĔX-ē-ăn) noun.

A person who can recite the alphabet backwards ("Z, y, x . . .") as quickly as forwards.
(coinage inspired by a word a the other end of the alphabet: *abecedarian* [ā-bē-sē-DAIR-ē-ăn], "one who teaches or learns the alphabet; a beginner"—*Webster*)
Coined by the author.

No dictionary worthy of the name would be complete without at least one word beginning with Z, the letter that lets you know things are coming to an end. And yet, believe it or not, Z was not always at the end of the alphabet. It comes from *zeta* which was and still is the sixth letter of the Greek alphabet. When the Romans adopted the Greek alphabet, they had no words using *zeta* and so they dropped it. Later on, as the Roman Empire and Latin language expanded, the Romans discovered they needed *zeta* after all and so they revived it and stuck it at the end of the alphabet.

It's been there ever since. And it's a popular spot for anyone who likes to come last:

WHAT'S ZZZUP?

According to a certain Mr. Turner's answering service, his assumed name of I. Zzzup was designed to get him the last listing in the Toronto telephone book. He was outzedded, however, by Shannon Zzzyk ("That number is no longer in service"), and by Zzzzoom Toys and Games ("I'm sorree . . .").

If it's any consolation, Mr. Turner, you have the last *working* number in the book. . . .

Incidentally, the last name in the Manhattan directory is Zweisel & Co. No imagination at all. [*The City, Toronto Star*, March 12, 1978.]

And now for the final curtain on the first edition of *Brave New Words*. It is only fitting that we should close with a word that will always be the last entry in any dictionary. . . .

Brave New Words at a glance

Many of the entries in *Brave New Words* have sprinted to victory in the Annual Dictionary Sweepstakes on the island of Lexiconia. The current winners by category are:

The longest word: *masticambulistiphile*
The shortest word: *et*
The hottest word: *pyropecuniac*
The coldest word: *ugloo*
The quickest word: *plumbiped*
The clammiest word: *oysterical*
The sexiest word: a toss-up between *sexophile* and *fornicatorium*
The sleepiest word: *yawnee*
The sloppiest word: *bioopsy*
The hairiest word: *omnibrow*, followed closely by *fuzztache* and *cybrow*
The baldest word: *baldephobia*
The loudest word: *g'orch!*
The hungriest word: a tie between *blupper* and *brunner*
The deadliest word: *bugicide*
The most appetizing word: *menuographer*
The most indigestible word: *bicyclivore*
The most alarming word: *bladderclock*
The most prehistoric word: *meanderthal*
The most expensive word: *cabloop*
The most intimate word: *covivant*
The most invisible word:
The most reversible word: *foof*
The most painful word: *impactipediphobia*
The most reproductive word: *crotchocrat*
The most intoxicated word: *omnibibulous*

170 Brave New Words at a glance

The most sinful word: *pwelgas*
The most punctuated word: *quiz?bang!*
The most metric word: *klickage*, with runners-up *dek, hek,* and *litrage*
The most shocking word: *riggafrutch!*
The most bombastic word: *sherkquacious*
The most useful word: *sesquilingual*
The most sinister word: *sinistrologist*
The most musical word: *g'orch*
The most embarrassing word: *tonguetipitis*
The most acrobatic word: *umbrellabat*
The most erotic word: *unikini*
The first word: *alphadef*
The last word: *zedwyexian*
The winningest word: *g'orch!* (for placing first in two categories—"loudest" and "most musical")

For Further Reading

If *Brave New Words* has turned you into an incurable lover of words both old and new, you'll want to feast your eyes upon the following books as soon as possible:

BARING-GOULD, WILLIAM S. *The Lure of the Limerick.* London: Panther Books, 1970.

BARNETT, LINCOLN. *The Treasure of Our Tongue.* New York: Alfred A. Knoff, 1964.

BARNHART, CLARENCE L., ed. *The Barnhart Dictionary of New English Since 1963.* New York: Barnhart/Harper & Row, 1973.

EHRLICH, IDA. *Instant Vocabulary.* New York: Pocket Books, 1968.

ERNST, MARGARET S. *More About Words.* New York: Alfred A. Knopf, 1951.

ESPY, WILLARD R. *An Almanac of Words at Play.* New York: Clarkson N. Potter, Inc., 1975.

ESPY, WILLARD R. *O Thou Improper, Thou Uncommon Noun.* Toronto: General Publishing, 1979.

FUNK, PETER. *It Pays to Increase Your Word Power.* New York: Bantam Books, Inc., 1970.

FUNK, WILFRED. *Six Weeks to Words of Power.* New York: Pocket Books, 1955.

FUNK, WILFRED and LEWIS, NORMAN. *30 Days to a More Powerful Vocabulary.* New York: Pocket Books, 1949.

FURNESS, EDNA. *Spelling for the Millions.* Toronto: Signet Books, 1964.

HENDRICKSON, ROBERT. *Human Words.* New York: Chilton Book Company, 1972.

KRASKE, ROBERT. *The Story of the Dictionary.* New York: Harcourt, Brace, Jovanovich, 1975.

LEWIS, NORMAN. *Word Power Made Easy.* New York: Doubleday & Company, Inc., 1949.

MORRIS, WILLIAM and MARY. *Harper Dictionary of Contemporary Usage.* New York: Harper & Row, 1975.

172 For Further Reading

MORRIS, WILLIAM. *Your Heritage of Words.* New York: Dell Publishing Co., Inc., 1970.

NURNBERG, MAXWELL and ROSENBLUM, MORRIS. *How to Build a Better Vocabulary.* New York: Popular Library, 1961.

SHIPLEY, JOSEPH T. *In Praise of English.* New York: Times Books, 1977.

SPERLING, SUSAN KELZ. *Poplollies and Bellibones.* New York: Clarkson N. Potter, Inc., 1977.

And last but not least, *Brave New Words, Volume Two* (now being written and to be filled with new words donated by the readers of *Brave New Words, Volume One*).

With Special Thanks

Behind every dictionary can be found the support and enthusiasm of countless individuals—and *Brave New Words* is no exception. I salute Lloyd Duncan and Marian Moore of York University's Centre for Continuing Education and Doug Stewart of the Toronto Public Libraries for helping me to launch my Word Power course, out of which sprouted the idea for this book. Over one thousand students have enrolled in Word Power since it first began at the Glendon Campus of York University in the spring of 1974. For me, these students—from all ages and backgrounds—have been a constant source of inspiration and delight in my search for new words.

My History students at North Toronto Collegiate Institute (where I now teach) and Northern Secondary School (where I taught for 10 years) have also contributed enormously to the birth of *Brave New Words*. Many of these students have coined words which are now breaking into print for the first time anywhere. Other students of mine, by pointing out definitions for which no word as yet existed, have been directly responsible for many of the new words I have coined myself. And others—David Atwood, Roland Drake, Helen Ferrigan, and many more—deserve special mention for the sheer enthusiasm they have displayed for words both old and new.

Many of my colleagues at both these Toronto high schools have also leaped aboard the lexicographical bandwagon. At North Toronto Collegiate Institute, Gerry Dunlevie and Don McNeill gave me valuable information on Latin and Greek roots; Bob Brown came up with the title *Brave New Words*; Hal Brown served as historical advisor on the missing Saxon kingdom of *Norsex*; Bob Boldt kept digging up *old* words I had never heard of before; John Hill read the entire manuscript the day before he flew to England; David Ford coined the only entry with an apostrophe (*g'orch*); Bob Krueger supplied a new swear word (*riggafrutch*); Lynn McMurray came up with a new term for people stuck in the suburbs (*siberbia*); Des Ottley and Dave Wallace coined new words for people who like to eat (*spork* and *lupper* respectively); Stew Passmore began calling my 1940 McLaughlin-Buick a *McCuik*; Paul Robert turned my surname into a verb (*sherking*: searching for new words); Victor Popov drew my attention to *hemidemisemiquavers* (see *duodemilingual*); and Bill Barker assisted with the proofreading (he would have helped with the editing too, but had to fly to England to work on his Ph.D.).

My colleagues during the 10 years I spent at Northern Secondary School

174 With Special Thanks

were equally helpful. Walter Cebrynsky and Bob Putnam arranged for me to teach a special Word Power unit as part of a new interdisciplinary credit course; "Champagne Charlie" Chinchen constantly regaled me with a flamboyant style of spoken English which can only be described as Chinchenian; Dom DiStasi ("the greatest Italian printer since Bodoni") coined *inverlegablist* for printers who can read backwards or upside-down; Harold Lass read the manuscript when it was only 50 pages long and said, "Keep going! Keep going!"; Bruno Scinto used his fascination for unusual words (especially *boustrophedon* and *infundibular*) to convince me there was a market for *Brave New Words*; Graham Walker provided me with the perfect ending for the *foulese* chapter; and Bob Warren not only coined *cabloop*—he also conversed with me one day in fractured French which prompted me to coin *sesquilingual*, my first new word.

Others who read the manuscript and offered valuable advice include Ted Beverley, a recent graduate of the Centennial College book publishing course in Toronto, four members of the Paterson family (Alan, Cathy, Carole, and Michael) while vacationing at their summer home on Lake Simcoe, Lew and Gwen Resnick (word lovers from 'way back), and Canadian poet John Robert Colombo, that "Master Gatherer" who has edited over one hundred books and written, compiled, or translated 20 others, including the highly acclaimed *Colombo's Canadian Quotations* and *Colombo's Canadian References*. Flip back to *tonguetipitis* to see Colombo in action.

Special thanks also go to Earl and Jim Domm, Dale and Dennis Fawcett, Rick Kollins, Maldwyn Williams, and Joe Solomon—all of Toronto—who offered their advice and encouragement. For publicity that generated an avalanche of letters from Canadians from coast to coast, a special tip of the hat goes to William French of the Toronto *Globe and Mail*, Helen Hutchinson of CTV's *Canada AM*, Bob McLean of the CBC-TV *Bob MacLean Show*, and Mary Virtue, librarian at Ryerson Polytechnical Institute in Toronto who offered *Brave New Words* as one of the prizes in her Cross-Canada Metric Word Contest (see *klickage*). And for those whose new words do not appear in this book, don't despair! There's plenty of room in *Brave New Words, Volume Two* (now being written).

I am indeed fortunate in having this book illustrated by the very talented Leah Taylor, a Grade 12 student at North Toronto Collegiate Institute. I was looking for an illustrator who can draw the way I write—and Leah fits the bill perfectly.

And finally, a very special salute to Rick Archbold, my editor at Doubleday Canada, for guiding the manuscript from my typewriter to the shelves of your favourite bookstore!

Word Card

Bill Sherk
c/o Doubleday Canada Limited
105 Bond St.
Toronto, Ontario
Canada M5B 1Y3

Date: _____

Dear Bill:
I have coined a word for the next edition of *Brave New Words* and here it is:

_____

Pronunciation: _____

Definition: _____

_____

Origin: _____

Usage in sample sentence: _____

_____

_____

Additional comments: _____

_____

_____

Coiningly yours,

Name: _____

Address: _____

_____